Twice Told Tombigbee Tales

Twice Told Tombigbee Tales

෨ · ෫

Michael P. Mills

BENCH CHIEF PAPERS
OXFORD, MISSISSIPPI

Copyright ©2007 by Michael P. Mills

All rights reserved.
No part of this book may be reproduced in any form
or by any electronic, photographic, or mechanical
means, including information storage and retrieval
systems, without permission in writing from
the publisher, except by a reviewer, who may quote
brief passages in a review.

Design and production supervision provided by
Quail Ridge Press
P. O. Box 123
Brandon, MS 39042
ISBN-13: 978-1-934193-03-7
ISBN-10: 1-934193-03-8

Cover painting by Lee Waddle • Oxford, Mississippi.

Manufactured in the United States of America.
First printing, March 2007 • Second, May 2007

BENCH CHIEF PAPERS
211 South 5th Street
Oxford, Mississippi 38655
benchchief@hotmail.com

Contents

Preface 7
Opening Statement 11
Ben Jones 21
I'm Gonna Be A Diamond Some Day 41
Preachin,' Prayin' and Politickin' 51
The Three Kings of Tombigbee Country 68
The Sun-N-Sand Years 77
The Life and Times of
    A. C. "Butch" Lambert, Sr. 111
Another Gentleman From Itawamba 137
When Heaven and Earth Pass 160
Armis 172
Literacy and Hawg Hunting 190
Nine-One-One 202
A Few Final Words 214

Preface

Mike Mills is a federal district judge, well-trained in the law, and like many barristers, a student of human nature. His particular gift as a writer is to see human nature as it has expressed itself in a special place and time. "We are products of place as much as chance," he writes, and he proceeds to illuminate the culture and life of his native northeast Mississippi. This region is an understudied place but a fascinating one. Geographically, it is the foothills of the Appalachian Mountain chain, with a culture dominated historically by yeoman farmers. In the nineteenth century, they were part of the Southern upcountry, the often isolated hilly areas that included north Georgia and north Alabama, into middle Tennessee and northern Arkansas. Far removed from the rich lands of the plantation belt, the upcountry was home to sturdy farmers who originally raised their own food crops and grazed livestock.

These were independent folks, and among the jewels of their culture was a sharp sense of humor. Storytelling came easily, and outsiders drew from it in creating the literary genre called Southwestern Humor, which flourished in the three decades before the Civil War. August Baldwin Longstreet, George Washington Harris, William Tappan Thompson, and Johnson Jones Hooper were just a few of the writers who produced sketches and short stories describing horse trades, dances, gander pullings, fights, shooting matches, and horse races that were typical fare in the newly opened areas of Alabama, Mississippi, and Arkansas that were then known as the Southwest. The narrators of Southwestern humor were typically literate gentlemen who tell of their encounters with rough-acting, dialect-speaking characters. This was a literature of the frontier, backwoods humor, but the rural South would long retain features of a Southern frontier, well into the twentieth century. William Faulkner was one Mississippian who wrote of the "plain folk" he saw around him in the early and mid-twentieth century, drawing from the humor of rural life.

Mike Mills's triumph is to return to the people who are descendants of that streak of rural humor, specifically as seen in northeast Mississippi. Unlike his nineteenth century literary ancestors, he is not distant from the people about whom he writes. Indeed, he intends his book to pay tribute to them. And they are a colorful lot—gentle but demanding schoolteachers, shrewd lawyers, down home hog hunters from bottomlands, inspirational coaches, and politicians everywhere. Mills writes of growing up in northeast Mississippi at a time when the effects and the memory of the Great

Depression were still tangible, into the modernization of the area, with people moving from a mixed farm economy of subsistence agriculture, small patches of cotton, and truck crops for sale in town to an economy of small factories and commerce. Mills's generation lived through the transformation of his home region, but it retained considerable continuity of values despite social and economic changes. His memories of living in a racially divided world and of the role of sports in desegregation are powerful evocations of the time of his youth.

This book is also the portrait of the attorney as a young man. He grew up among decent people and took their values with him into his political campaigning, which led to service in the legislature and then on the Mississippi Supreme Court. His level-headedness keeps him from succumbing to the temptations of the legislative lifestyle that he observes and documents, but his tales of the Sun-N-Sand Motel, of attending country church services as an aspiring politician, and of the characters of the Mississippi political world are often hilarious and always insightful about Southern political life.

Mills has written a memoir that is far more than that. It documents the storytelling culture of northeast Mississippi in a way no one has done before and it offers a revealing inside view of Mississippi political life over the last two decades. Mills is a sharp observer of people and places, a man of scholarly bent who can put what he sees into broad perspective of other people and other places. Above all, though, this is a witty book. You'll slap your knees when you read about Sut-N-Goober from the bottomlands and the many other folks who jump off the pages of this finely-crafted book.

Charles Reagan Wilson
University of Mississippi

Opening Statement

The clear branches of Tishomingo and the muddy creeks of Prentiss join near the little community of Ryan's Well in Itawamba County to form the East Fork of the old Tombigbee River where it begins its meandering journey through northeast Mississippi and west Alabama, headed to the Gulf Coast. Tributary names of the old Tombigbee whisper hints of our past. Mackey, Donivan, Bourland, Reed and English Creeks name some of our founding families. My maternal ancestors dug Dulaney branch which becomes Cummings Creek in Fulton just before it dips into the Tombigbee. Little Wolf and Panther Creeks have obvious connotations. Lick Skillet Creek speaks of hard times for the early settlers. And our native-American heritage is never far from memory with creek, town and county names such as Boguefala, Boguegaba, Mantachie, Chickasaw and Tishomingo.

My earliest memories reach back to Sandy Springs Baptist Church near the headwaters of the Tombigbee in Ryan's Well where my ancestors lived for generations. I got a good dose of old time religion and a healthy fear of the Almighty from early sermons and revivals at Sandy Springs. I remember standing outside Dwight Jamerson's barber shop one afternoon when I was five or six, waiting for my Daddy to get his hair cut. I had just gotten a fresh flat-top and was studying the clouds passing overhead. At one point all the clouds seemed to swirl into a never-ending funnel reaching higher and higher into the sky. The interior of the funnel blazed with vivid colors. Red and yellow and purple and gold. It may have been the sunset. It may have been something else. I was awestruck by the vast beauty. I thought I saw Jacob's Ladder ascending into heaven. I was, at that moment, struck by an awareness of something, some one, far greater than myself. I would not have this same feeling again for a long, long time to come.

Other memories include standing beside the old North Road, which was graveled then, waiting for Melvin Steele's peddler truck to come by so I could buy a Baby Ruth candy bar for a nickel. Tales of mad dogs roaming the roads and panthers in the hills were still common in my childhood days in Ryan's Well. Trips across the river on the old wooden bridge at Walker's Levee kept me in touch with my Guin's kin across the river. Such trips are no longer possible since the new Tennessee-Tombigbee Waterway split Itawamba in half, leaving us with only one bridge at Fulton.

My family left our little farm in Ryan's Well when I was six or seven years old. We moved downstream to Fulton where we joined the good solid folks who worshiped at East Fulton Missionary Baptist Church. Many folks at East Fulton, especially the women, played a part in shaping my early values and sense of place. Our preacher's wife, Faye Ellen Digby, comes to mind. Miss Faye Ellen, as we called her, was a model of grace and good humor for our little band of Baptists. She had a knack for making everyone feel special. (She still does.) And many other women did too: Miss Mildred Wilson, Miss Juanita Martin, Miss Pauline Walton, Miss Martha Wallace, Miss Capitola Bowman, Miss Esther Sheffield, Miss Jane Guntharp, Miss Jo Bates, Miss Billie Spradling and others come to mind. Thanks to their patience, those of us who attended Vacation Bible School at East Fulton became fairly fluent in Biblical matters and ping-pong. (Miss Faye Ellen's husband, Brother Eugene, was a world-class ping-pong player.) And they led by example.

I recall Miss Eva Lois Johnson. Her special gift is cooking and she always prepared something special for the shut-ins and the sick, for those grieving, or for visiting preachers or just because she wanted to surprise someone. Her specialty is chicken-and-dumplings but she also makes a delicious coconut pie. (By the way, the ladies of Itawamba County make the best coconut pies in the South. They also make the best slaw. I know because I have tried slaw and coconut pies from Tremont to Tulsa. The next time you are in the Country Gentleman outside Fulton, try their slaw and have a piece of coconut pie. I think you will agree with me.)

I had graduated from Vacation Bible School when I

took a job at Joe's Pak-N-Sak, a small grocery store in Fulton. Oxford attorney Mike Watts worked in the Pak-N-Sak meat market when I was the sack-boy. Thursdays were our busy days when Blue Bell let out and the ladies who made their living all day, every day sewing a left pants pocket on every pair of blue jeans coming down the line came in just after three o'clock and grabbed a shopping cart and began racing down the aisles, anxious to get the specials and a week's supply of essentials and then beat the school busses home so they would be there for their children. We had an old free-standing microphone in the "front office" which we used as a primitive public address system. When the full shopping carts got about three deep at the counter and I began to get behind, I "got on the mike" and said, "Mr. Watts. Come up front please. Need some help sacking groceries."

My perch at the end of the check-out counter exposed me to people from all over the county. Small farmers and salesmen, school teachers and county officials. I developed empathy for the working people, especially the working women who spent nearly a week's wages on food and necessities for their families, often cashing their little checks to pay for the groceries, with little change left over.

One of my favorite customers was Rosabel Burleson, known to everyone in Fulton as 'Honey.' Honey was a beautiful blonde who grew up in Electric Mills, Mississippi where her mother ran a boarding house and her father worked for the railroad. Honey and her

Delta State football hero husband, Big Bill Burleson, moved to Fulton during World War II where they reared three lovely daughters, Roseanne, Nancy and Angel, and two sons, Bill and Bob. Honey drove a candy-apple red Pontiac, was fond of opera and ran a day care center at her home. She cared for her 'day children' as well as she cared for her own.

For a number of years Honey heard me "get on the microphone" and say, "Mike, come up front. Need some help sacking groceries," as she approached the counter with her two carts full of day-care provisions. She often said I had a "lovely voice."

Over the years, politics and law have toughened my skin considerably. I have had to make a few hard decisions, some of which have not been particularly popular. Consequently, I have occasionally borne a bit of criticism. (Much of it well-deserved I must confess.) Having endured public second-guessing for many years now, I no longer worry much about what politicians or preachers or lawyers or newspaper editors say about me. I realize they are just doing their jobs, too. But if I thought I was disappointing Miss Faye Ellen or Miss Eva Lois or Honey Bee.... well, that is a different matter altogether.

I graduated from high school and enrolled in Itawamba Community College. The following summer found me working for Jesco, a Fulton contracting company with jobs spread across North Mississippi. I was assigned to George Martin's crew, building the Trace-Way Manor Nursing Home in Tupelo. I spent most of that hot summer digging a hole eighteen inches deep and twelve inches wide, wherever George pulled the string, or pushing a screet board through hot concrete till my legs turned green.

Our crew had some fine characters. Vester Pettigo ran the back-hoe and gave me a lot of good advice. A fellow named George Zaviski from Eastern Europe (who had about a dozen kids) taught me a lot about using a pick and a shovel. I liked the work and I liked the workers and I liked George.

We had a small office with a phone on the job site. The only person who ever received calls was George. (We looked forward to phone calls since George would have to go inside the office to take the call and we could ease up a bit till he returned.) One day the phone rang and George patiently stepped over strings and ditches and re-bar as he headed toward the office and disappeared inside and we eased up a bit. He had a puzzled look on his face when he returned. "Mike, that call was for you. Johnny Crane. Said he wanted you to call him when you get back to Fulton this afternoon." Mr. Pettigo and Mr. Zaviski looked at me in a new light. I was the first person other than George to ever receive a call on the job, and from Johnny Crane, nonetheless.

Everyone in Fulton knew and knows Johnny Crane. He and his father, F.L., and brother Jimmy started their sub-contracting specialty firm in the late 1950's in Itawamba County with little more than a pickup truck, a wheel barrow and a shovel. Their business soon grew to regional, and later national, import.

Opening Statement

After the phone call, I was anxious to learn why Johnny Crane needed to get in touch with a Jesco hole-digger like me. Several possibilities ran through my mind. None were particularly encouraging. The hours seemed like days as the afternoon work dragged on. Finally we finished for the day and I and the other workers piled into the back of George's red Jesco pick-up and headed home for Fulton.

I called Johnny as soon as I could. He asked who I was supporting for governor in that year's election. I suspected I did not have the correct answer to his question. I offered that William Winter and Maurice Dantin seemed like nice guys to me. Johnny replied that he was "backing a fellow named Cliff Finch" and that Cliff had asked him to "find someone to speak on his behalf in North Mississippi."

I was flattered but a bit confused. I had never made a public speech in my life, other than reciting a few verses in Vacation Bible School. At the time I was wrestling with the idea of going full-time into construction work rather than finishing college. My plans did not include getting involved in a governor's race. I was willing to give it a try but first wanted to know, "how did you come up with my name?"

"I asked Honey Burleson who she would recommend and she said you were a good public speaker," Johnny replied. Little did Johnny know that the speeches Honey had heard were all spoken over the Joe's Pak-N-Sak loud-speaker.

That summer, Johnny and I worked rallies and

speakings all over the State. I would get out my Cliff Finch lunch box and Johnny would grab a handful of brochures and "work" the crowd while I spoke. I don't remember anything significant about my speeches other than "Cliff was for the working man" and "Cliff Finch . . . rhymes with wrench." These lines seemed to please the crowds. And doggone if Cliff didn't win.

That was my introduction to politics and public life. The same year, I married my high school sweetheart, the green eyed beauty Mona Robinson. Today, Mona and I have four fine children, Alysson, Chip, Rebekah and Penn. Rearing four children and now, our silly but wise family pet, Rupert the Wheatable, have given Mona and me many growth opportunities. And someday I may tell these tales. But for now I wish to share the stories of the folks who, like the women of East Fulton, Honey Burleson and Johnny Crane, made and make life in the Tombigbee hills special.

A special thanks is owed to friends who helped me put these words on paper. To Clyde Wilson at *Tombigbee Country Magazine* who first published some of my stories. To Beth Weinhouse for her patient advice and to David Galef for his tireless and unrewarded promotion of my efforts. To Charles Reagan Wilson for his encouragement and gentle spirit. To my mother Shirley, who always believed.

The people and events I sketch are colored by bits of song and scraps of faith, and tempered, usually, by innate good humor. You will notice that many times I am simply relating the tales of others for you.

Tombigbee folk are good story tellers. People from other parts of the country may have many choices among which to be entertained. The opera. Broadway. Baseball games. Museums. Those of us from the Tombigbee hills lacked such options growing up. So we entertained ourselves. By telling stories. These stories of people and events I have known are gifts from them to me to you.

We preserve the past through stories. I write to speak, in a fashion, with a great-grandchild or time-distant niece or nephew or some little cousin, or maybe a friend, whom I shall never know in this life, but whom I love already. That you may know something of the fellows and folk who toted it down the road a bit for you. And lived and loved along the way. Folks who made do and did the best they could with the snatches of life they found around them. That you may pick up the burden, and with a knowing chuckle and kind heart, help another along the way.

Michael P. Mills
Spring 2007

Ben Jones

Ben David Jones has lived his life beating tough odds. He was born in the little town of Hatley in Monroe County in 1930, the son of a disabled logger. Ben's father owned a one-horse wagon, which they rode to Amory on Saturday mornings, hauling truck-patch vegetables to sell for a little cash. That little boy today stands taller than six feet. With time, his shock of thick black hair has turned salt-and-pepper gray. His face is highlighted by a chronic good-natured smile and dancing blue eyes, which seem to say, "Hey, you and I know something that no one else knows." That's what Ben says when he has something clever to say. "Hey." When he gets excited or irritated, he will say, "Hoo! Hoo!" That is Benspeak for cussing. His soft voice, not marked by any particular dialect, is well suited for explaining. He rarely yells. He is a coach for life.

High school football in Fulton, Mississippi, changed forever one Friday night in 1967 when Coach Jones put Roy Lee Creighton into a game. Something else, bigger than football, changed too.

Football was the center of our world when I was

growing up in Itawamba County. Nothing competed with the sport for communal love and affection. High school football is a religion throughout the South and Ben David Jones, head coach of the Itawamba Agricultural High School Indians, was our high priest. Worshipful fans filled the old Itawamba Junior College Stadium on Friday nights to watch our boys battle Booneville and Baldwyn and Ripley and our other North Mississippi neighbors for bragging rights in the old Tombigbee Conference. The Itawamba Indians won their share of titles in the 1960's and the 1970's under Coach Jones. But Ben did more than just win championships. He taught us how to live. To accept ourselves and others for who we were. Regardless of caste or color. Ben was into reconciliation before it was cool.

Most Mississippi public schools did not integrate until 1969. However our local leaders decided that integration was the law of the land and that they would fully integrate all twelve grades in 1967 without waiting for a Federal court order.

Integration in the South was not easy for whites or blacks. Not all black parents were happy about sending their children to the white schools and most whites weren't thrilled about the idea either. We tend to forget that in most cases the black communities saw their neighborhood schools closed and it was the black teachers and administrators who lost their jobs when integration was fully implemented.

Coach Jones and our high school principal, Mr. Wayne Woods met with parents of the black children in the summer of 1967 to assure them their children would be safe in the formerly white public schools and that their children would enjoy the same opportunities as the white children when the fall semester began. Of course Ben encouraged the parents to let the black kids try out for the football team.

When fall practice began, 87 boys tried out for football. Eighteen were black and had never played a down of organized football. One of the black kids was a six-foot six-inch, 275-pound sophomore named Roy Lee Creighton.

Ben Jones has a philosophy in coaching (and life) which he calls "The Fairness Principle." The Fairness Principle dictates that the best eleven players on the team will start, regardless of status or color. Everyone has a chance to prove himself. If a young man thinks he should be starting at a given position, he tells the coach and is allowed to challenge the starter for his posi-

Coach Ben Jones and Tombigbee Conference Championship Trophy

tion. The best player gets the job. I use the fairness principle in law. If a legal issue is close and both sides seem equally adamant about the law, and it is hard to determine which side is right, under the law, I have found it helpful to just fall back on the fairness principle in making my decision. I have found few who can argue with this approach.

Word went around town that Ben was letting black kids on the team. A group of concerned white parents went to complain to the principal, Mr. Woods. He told them he was standing behind the coach. They then went to see Ben. He explained his Fairness Principle and told them the best eleven players would start, regardless of color. Some of the parents then stated that they wanted separate dressing rooms and showers for the white players. Ben said that wouldn't do. The players had the option of using the same facilities or not using any at all. In fact, Ben says, the black kids didn't use the common showers when they first began practice. There was too much tension on the team.

After the first hot summer practice, Ben told the boys to run what he called his "Victory Lap" around the field. The players were halfway around the field when, according to Ben, "Roy Lee Creighton just fell out. Like he was dead. I blew my whistle to stop the others. He was out of breath but OK. I told him to get up and finish the run because everyone else was going to have to run until he completed his lap. But he wouldn't get up. The boys got after him pretty good but he just lay there like he was dead until everyone else left the field."

The next day after practice, Ben again told the boys to do a Victory Lap. About halfway around the field, according to Ben, "Roy Lee fell out again. This time I didn't blow the whistle. I just said, 'Boys, everybody has to finish the lap.' Some of the boys turned and surrounded Roy Lee. Hey, they got on him pretty good again. I couldn't see what they were doing, but they must have been pretty rough on him. After a while they got him up and he staggered on around the field.

"After about ten days of this, I put a small baby bottle filled with milk in my pocket. After practice, I told the boys to do a Victory Lap. Sure enough, about halfway around the field, Roy Lee just fell out like he was dead!"

Ben blew his whistle and all the boys trotted over to Roy Lee, who lay stretched out on the ground. Ben said, "Roy Lee, do you know what I'm gonna do to you?"

Roy Lee opened one eye, squinted up at Ben, and said, "You gonna yell at me and let them kick me again and treat me real bad?"

Ben said, "No, Roy Lee. I got something for you." He handed the baby bottle to Roy Lee.

Roy Lee sat up, screwed the top off the bottle, drank the milk, wiped his mouth, handed the bottle back to Ben and said, "Thanks, Coach, you got any more?"

The players, white and black, exploded with laughter! At Ben. Roy Lee had broken the tension. As we say in North Mississippi, Roy Lee had "gotten the best" of Ben. That afternoon everyone showered together. They were becoming a team.

The players had overcome their differences. But noone knew how the community would react if Ben put a black player on the field. No black had ever played any sport in the Tombigbee Conference.

The racial code of segregated education in Itawamba County before 1967 was simply a local reflection of what we knew as "The Southern Way of Life." This way of life rested upon the twin pillars of racial separation, *de jure* and *de facto*.

De jure means "of the law." In 1896, the U.S. Supreme Court ruled in the Louisiana case of *Plessy v. Ferguson* that the State of Louisiana could order people of color to ride in separate railroad cars from whites. This decision underpinned all Southern laws mandating separation of the races, particularly in education, for another six decades.

The law can be changed with the stroke of a pen. Behavior may be enforced at the point of a bayonet. Habits of mind do not surrender so easily. *De facto* segregation was segregation in fact, whether lawful or not. *De facto* segregation was based upon habit . . . custom . . . tradition. *De facto* segregation was shaped by business relationships, religious practices, family mores and education. *De facto* segregation was learned.

Itawamba County, the second whitest county in the State, was not a hot-bed of resistance to Federal law in the 1960's. Neither were we untouched by the forces of change.

I remember separate water fountains at the county courthouse and the timid way black folks approached white folks on the sidewalk. I remember poll taxes and, of course, all-white class rooms. Segregation, however, was not limited to public matters. No laws that I recall mandated that blacks and whites worship separately. Yet integrated worship services were unthinkable in the Mississippi I knew as a child.

Law, custom and religion taught us that blacks were inferior, and few great souls saw otherwise.

I don't recall when I first heard of Martin Luther King, Jr. I do remember that the only person I knew who respected him was my mother, Shirley. Most other adults would react to his appearance in the newspapers or on television with anger or ridicule. Children imitate their parents. We had a recess chant in Grammar School, where some kids would gleefully sing "All I want is my civil rights" as they dragged a leg behind, pretending to be shackled to a ball and chain. Of course, I laughed along with everyone else.

A rather simple incident occurred in 1964 to first prick my consciousness about race. We had been on a family vacation to Panama City in Daddy's white Chevrolet Impala. We were headed home on a two-lane highway somewhere south of Montgomery. I was sitting in the back seat with my brother Billy and sister Sharon. Baby sister Darlene was up front with Mother and Daddy. Our car didn't have an air conditioner so we were traveling with the windows down. I felt the car slow to a crawl and I heard Daddy say that there were "marchers up ahead." The Alabama Highway Patrol had pulled a long caravan of black people to the side of the road. They were headed to Montgomery.

Patrolmen were waving the white folks around the caravan. As we creeped along in the hot Alabama sunshine, I saw black men and women and children standing in family groups of four or five, patiently waiting for permission to travel. Most of the adults were talking and visiting or squatting in the shade of their old pickups and sedans. A few children were playing in the red ditch-banks cut just beyond the highway shoulders. Most of the men were dressed in worn overalls or plain work clothes, the women wearing simple cotton dresses. One small group was standing in a circle singing a familiar old hymn. At the time, it seemed out of place:

Walked over Jordan, what do I see . . .
comin' for to carry me home . . .

The music was strangely comforting. It had never occurred to me that they might worship with the same songs we used. And then I saw a simple act of love which has since clung to my mind like a moral stick-tight. As we eased past the singers, I spied a big black man in overalls, leaning back against the hood of an old green pickup, his full gray-speckled beard pointed toward heaven, as he smiled at the happy child he was gently rocking above his head. It was an act of love. I had seen my Daddy do the same thing with my little sister.

Not everyone had seen the light in 1967 when the Itawamba Indians were preparing for their first game of the season against Baldwyn. More than a ballgame was at stake. Coach Jones and our boys were facing a hundred years of *de jure* and *de facto* segregation. A week before the game, a few malcontents put out the word of what they would do to Ben Jones " if he lets one of them play." The police chief told Ben to take the threat seriously. He said, "Don't you put those black boys out there on that field. We have been told that they will get you if you let those black boys play." The Fairness Principle now faced a big test. Habits of hate are hardest to break.

Coach Jones never responded well to threats. Before the game, he called his players together and told them they were a team. That they had to stick together. And then he said, "Before the 'Star Spangled Banner' is played, I want all of you to walk completely around the field together. Without your helmets or your shoulder pads on. I want everybody here to see what color you are. Black or white. And I don't want anybody on this team to be ashamed of your color. 'Cause I'm not."

The boys did as they were told and walked silently around the field before the National Anthem was played. The one that talks about " the land of the free." The kids heard the silence in the stands.

No black kid started the game. Baldwyn led 7 to 0 at the half. The third quarter began and Baldwyn had the ball. It was a passing situation and Ben decided to put Roy Lee in the game. After all, he was the tallest kid on the team! Roy Lee trotted onto the field, the first black to play in a Tombigbee Conference football game, if not the first in the State of Mississippi. The stadium was silent a moment, then scattered boos were heard. Most folks waited to see what would happen. The ball was snapped. The Baldwyn quarterback dropped back to pass. He saw his receiver. He threw. Roy Lee stood and raised his arms as Coach Jones had taught him. He deflected the ball! It fell into the hands of his teammate Chuck Carpenter, who ran 35 yards for a touchdown.

The crowd went wild, shouting "Roy Lee! Roy Lee!" as the grinning young giant trotted off the field. In the next series Ben sent Hank Stone in as the second black to play in the Tombigbee Conference. He heard nothing but cheers. Fulton beat Baldwyn 28 to 7.

Race was never again an issue in Fulton football. The football team's success, based upon mutual respect between the races, spilled over into other parts of the community. Our small town closed the 1960's with little racial strife.

• • •

Itawamba was not Ben Jones' first successful venture into coaching. He began his head coaching career as head basketball coach at Gulfport in 1958. His resourcefulness became apparent when his team played for the Big-8 Championship in 1960. In the playoffs leading to the championship game, Yazoo City, coached by Cob Jarvis, had been defeated in the semi-finals by Jackson Murrah, which had a superior team. Jarvis told Ben that Gulfport could not beat Murrah if

Gulfport ever got two points behind. In those days there was no shot clock, and some teams would simply dribble and pass the ball to run out the clock once they got ahead. The only way to get the ball back was to commit a foul, and Murrah had excellent foul shooters. They rarely missed a free throw. The teams only got one shot for the first five fouls of each half. Thereafter, they got two shots for each foul.

In the championship game, Jackson Murrah lead Gulfport 16 to 12 at the half. A four point lead. It looked bad for Ben's boys. But Ben came up with a plan to win. As he says, "We were going to the dressing room and hey, a shining light went off in my head. We would foul them the first five times they got the ball to start the second half, preventing them from getting a two point shot and forcing them to have a chance at only one point. We would then score two for every one point they got, allowing us, with some luck, to start the second half with a ten to five run, thereby gaining a one point lead. Hey, it was worth a try."

The second half began and Gulfport intentionally fouled. The Jackson player missed the free throw! Gulfport scored! A two point lead. Jackson got the ball. Gulfport fouled. Jackson missed the free throw again! Gulfport scored two. The game was tied up. Same thing again. Same result. Gulfport now took the lead and would not relinquish it. Gulfport beat Jackson 40 to 35 to win the Big-8 title which, in those days, was equivalent to winning the state championship. Ben was selected Big-8 Basketball Coach of the Year.

From Gulfport, Ben and wife Bobbye and daughters Becky and Ginger moved to Tupelo, where he coached boy's basketball and was assistant football coach. Ben has a football drill where he stands the linemen in a circle, throws the ball up and makes them jump for it. Teaches the big boys agility. Mississippi Legislator Butch Lambert, whose son played on the team, was watching the boys practice this drill one day when he said, "You can tell he's a basketball coach. He's got jump ball on his mind all the time!"

The Tupelo Superintendent of Education offered Bobbye a job. She accepted and signed a contract. Just before school started, the Superintendent reneged on Bobbye's job. This didn't "set well" with Ben, who went to see a lawyer who told him, "You can make them honor her contract. But next year you and she both will be out of a job." Hey, a deal's a deal. Ben made them honor the contract. The next year they were both out of a job with two little girls to support.

Ben went looking for work. He took a break from job searching one day and stopped at the Dairy Kream in East Tupelo for a cone of ice cream. He struck up a conversation with the owner and not only bought an ice cream cone, he bought the dairy bar. He traded his unsold house in Gulfport for the business. Though he had never cooked a hamburger or mixed a milkshake, he mastered the art quickly and supported his family the next year as a short-order cook at the Dairy Kream.

One of Ben's best customers at the little dairy bar in East Tupelo was Delmus Harden, owner and editor of the *Itawamba County Times*, and an ice cream lover. In August of 1963, the head football coach at Fulton suffered a serious pre-season injury and was unable to coach. Delmus stopped by the Dairy Cream for some ice cream. He learned that Ben was out of a job and asked if he would be interested in a temporary position in Fulton. Ben said he would coach the boys until the other coach was able to return. He signed a three-week contract. The first game was in six days.

The Fulton boys didn't accept Ben at first. They loved their permanent coach, Billy Spigner, and didn't want to learn Ben's system. Likewise, he refused to learn theirs. So they did the best they could. They beat Baldwyn in the season opener and next tied Okolona, coached at the time by future Mississippi State Coach Bob Tyler. Ben tells me Fulton had a game-winning touchdown called back in that game. He never forgets anything.

The next week Ben got a contract extension for the remainder of the season. The Indians lost only one game that season, to Macon, and won the Tombigbee Conference championship. Ben was on his way to becoming a coaching legend. He had found a home.

Ben did more than just coach football in Fulton. He and Delmus began a jailhouse ministry. Each Sunday morning they would go to the Fulton jail and read scripture with the inmates. Ben says that their mission was primarily for the Lord, "but hey, you never know where you can pick up a good football player."

In 1966 Ben's team again won the conference championship. Mississippi didn't have football playoffs in those days; rather, the more successful teams were invited to play in bowl games. Fulton was invited to play Leflore County in the Grenada Lake Bowl. Ben believed in studying the opposition. He obtained the film of a game between Leflore County and Drew. He remembers today that Leflore beat Drew 67 to 34 in the game he watched. But he noticed that Drew had a great young quarterback who was quick and had a good arm.

In 1967 Ben was selected as an assistant coach of the North team in the Mississippi All-Star game. The designated head coach chose his quarterback for the All-Star team. Ben remembered the quarterback from Drew whom he had watched on film, so he lobbied for his selection as an All-Star too.

The pre-game camp was held on Millsaps campus. Ben says it was apparent that the kid from Drew had more talent than any of the other quarterbacks. The North head coach, however, was loyal to his quarterback, and selected him to start. The young man was injured after a few plays. Ben then said, "Hey, let's give that speckle-headed boy a chance." They put the young Archie Manning in the game. He lit up the scoreboard with seven touchdown passes. The North All-Stars won 57 to 34.

Ben's true genius rests in his ability to motivate others. He is a born psychologist. He has an instinct for rewarding good behavior. One of his tricks when I played football for him was the water drill, which occurred late in practice when everyone was tired. He would place the ball on the goal line and give the offense four chances to score on the defense. If the offense scored, they got a drink of water. If the defense held, they got the water. In a real game, you would hear our boys calling out, "No water on me," as they lined up for a goal line stand. It worked. In 1972, we gave up no goal line points.

Ben Jones had another motivational tool whereby he would "dedicate a game to mother." Surreptitiously Ben would have our mothers write a letter to us, telling us how proud she was that "you are an Indian" and how she knew we would give it everything we had to win the big game for her. Ben would then dedicate the biggest game of the season to our mothers. When we came to the dressing room before the game, each of us would find the letter from our mother in our locker. By game time, he would have us worked up into a crying frenzy to "go out there and win one for your mother!"

One of my favorite Indian teammates was a big, happy boy named Larry Brooks. Larry, the son of a Methodist minister, was one of the finest young men to ever graduate from Itawamba Agricultural High School. He was a great punter, running back and defensive back. He was also a gifted person. He was quick to defend others and had a soft spot in his heart for those of lesser means or those who came from difficult circumstances. Ben spotted Larry's potential when he was in the 10th grade. He told Larry that he might have a chance to play football in the Southeastern Conference but that he could not rely on natural talent alone. He must work hard to become stronger and faster.

Larry says, "I did work hard." Over the next three years Ben often would single Larry out in practice. When he missed a play, according to Larry, "He would tilt his head and turn his black cap sideways on his head and ask, 'Do you like getting run over? Hoo! Hoo!' or he would grin when you made a good play and ask, 'What do you think about that? Hoo! Hoo!' "

Another star on our 1972 team was my classmate and friend, Dale "Bonehead" Stone. Dale was the younger brother of Hank Stone, one of the first black players on the 1967 team. Dale was a three-year starter at running back and linebacker. He was one of the best athletes I have ever seen but he wasn't much of a motorcycle rider. Dale had a Honda 75 motorcycle which he had modified with a banana seat and Easy Rider handle bars. He was cruising through campus one Monday morning when he collided with the back end of a big yellow school bus which had stopped to unload students. He totaled his motorcycle, nearly bit his tongue in half and was severely bruised and banged up.

The doctors sewed Dale's tongue together and released him to go to school. We had a big game coming up Friday night against the Ripley Tigers, who were led by the future college All-American punter, Jim Miller, and the great All-State and future All-SEC running-back, James Storey. Dale declared himself unable to play because of his sore tongue and bruises. Ben said he understood but asked Dale to just put on his running shorts and cleats and come on out to the practice field with the team. Dale mumbled with his sore tongue, "O-thay, Coath."

We ran a few plays with a substitute in Dale's place. Ben then said, "Dale, get in there at linebacker and just stand in your position."

"O-thay, Coath."

We ran another play. Ben then told our manager, Mike Albert, now a doctor in Pearl, that he was concerned about Dale standing out there without a helmet. "Go get Dale's helmet and let him put it on." He did. We ran another play.

Ben then said, "Albert, I'm still concerned about Dale. Go get his shoulder pads and jersey." He did and Dale put them on.

We ran another play. Then Ben said, "Albert, go get his pants." He did. Dale put them on. Then Ben said, "Dale, how do you feel now?"

Dale grinned and said, "O-thay, Coath." He started the game and led us to a big victory at Ripley.

Our 1972 team went undefeated and untied and won Ben's seventh Tombigbee Conference Championship. We scored nearly 400 points and gave up only 23. Mississippi State signed Larry Brooks to a scholarship.

Larry was an instant star at State as a freshman. Tragically, his career ended too soon. He was making a tackle in spring practice in 1975 when something went wrong. Larry never got up from the play. He was taken from the practice field on a stretcher, his neck broken. He would remain hospitalized for several months.

Ben was attending a coaching clinic in Atlanta when he received the call about Larry. He headed for Mississippi. He found Larry paralyzed from his neck down. He wanted to comfort Larry in some way but found it hard to say anything. Larry was more interested in comforting Ben.

"Coach," he said. "When I went down, I knew I was hurt bad. When they got me on the stretcher, I looked around as best I could and I saw a man sitting up in the stands in a red shirt and a black cap. I thought it was you! So I waved my finger to let you know that I wasn't going to give up. That I'm gonna make it. And Coach, I am gonna make it."

Larry's prognosis wasn't good. He had no grip in his hands and he couldn't move his legs. The doctors told him he would likely never walk again. But the doctors weren't aware of his work ethic. Larry Brooks knew he would have to work hard to walk again or even lift a spoon. But hey, he had worked hard before. After several months in the hospital and several more months of grueling physical therapy, Larry Brooks learned to walk again. Soon enough, he could use his arms and hands, too. The first thing he did when he became ambulatory was get in his daddy's car and drive himself to Meridian, where Ben was then coaching. He pulled up to Ben's house and blew the horn. When Ben came out, Larry got out of his car and staggered toward him, to show his coach he could walk again.

Ben left us in 1973 to become head football coach at Itawamba Junior College. He built a championship program there and later did the same at Meridian and New Albany. Many reasons have been argued for his success. One of his former assistant coaches, Paul Johnson has been quoted as saying, "There are fewer mental errors under Jones, because he won't hesitate to bench the offender." According to Johnson, Ben also worked hard on the finer points of the game, such as kicking and punt coverage. "As a result of this concentration, he's never had a punt blocked in all his years of coaching." Johnson said that Ben put everything he had into the game. "It's a way of life, there is no half way. Jones doesn't know how to lose . . . but when he does, he blames himself, not his players."

I have observed many coaches over the years. Few have been as successful as Ben Jones. And fewer have been as adored by their players. There is a reason for this. Ben cared for his players as persons first, and then as athletes. He wanted to affect your life. Too many coaches today are interested only in piling up wins and climbing the coaching ladder. You don't hear from these guys once you leave the program. Not so with Ben. I have never run for public office without his advice and help. He has been my lifetime coach and cheerleader. When I was campaigning for the legislature and the Supreme Court, Ben spent Friday nights handing out campaign literature for me at high school football games. Hey, it was competition, wasn't it?

Ben has retired from coaching, but he hasn't retired from life. He is active in the American Legion, the Forty and Eight, and serves as President of the

Mississippi County Forestry Association. Every fall he hands out thousands of American flags to first-graders in Northeast Mississippi schools and every spring he plants thousands of pine tree seedlings. Jacque Thrash, one of Ben's veteran friends, says that soon after a recent storm, he and Ben drove out to inspect eighty acres of newly planted pine trees. Some of the little seedlings had been blown to the ground. Jacque says he and Ben walked the entire eighty acres, straightening the little trees, because, as Ben told him, "Many of these trees may not make it anyway, but some of them will grow crooked if they aren't straightened. We can at least give them a chance by taking the time to straighten them now." Ben knows that young people need the same guidance.

Every young person who ever played for Ben learned something positive from him. I learned to expect not miracles, but results. I learned to respect others for their abilities and not for their color or status in life. I also learned to appreciate, in his words, the value "of things as they exist and what it means to be a free and independent individual . . . the courage to hold my head high . . . and defy the criticism of others when you know you are right . . . to know when to choose between right and wrong . . . that there is a God . . . and that he is ever-present."

They oughta name somethin' in Fulton after the man.

I'm Gonna Be a Diamond Some Day

One afternoon Grady Tollison, an Oxford lawyer and regional bon vivant who grew up in Tippah (pronounced Tipper) County, paid a visit to my Capitol office in Jackson. I was the new Chairman of the Judiciary "A" Committee in the Mississippi House of Representatives, and Grady was the new President of the Mississippi Bar. Though we had been friends for several years, Grady's visit was more than a mere social call. He was taking care of business. My committee had oversight responsibilities over the Mississippi Bar, and both of us were keenly aware of this circumstance. Candidly, we were also enjoying the chance to refer to each other by our recently acquired titles as "Mr. President" and "Mr. Chairman." We had enjoyed a bit of small talk when Grady asked me what I considered, at the time, a profound question:

> Mr. Chairman, who has had the biggest influence on your life? Can you name a specific person who made a difference in who you are?

I interpreted the question to imply, of course, that I had now made it. Like any politician, I was flattered to be asked such a question (as I suspect he intended) and, the question having been put, found myself quite willing to expound on the evolution of Mr. Chairman Mike Mills.

I pondered Grady's query a moment or so, thinking of many who had positively influenced my life, and one or two who had not. Family members came to mind first. My mother and daddy, who did the best they could to see that all their children were fed and clothed and attended church every time the doors opened. I thought of other kin, such as my Grandpa Mills, a country blacksmith, who made me a little wooden goat wagon for my fifth birthday. I could completely disassemble the wagon and put it back together all by myself. I spent many hours pulling my little brother Billy around the small farm we lived on near Sandy Springs in north Itawamba County. Grandpa Mills died too soon—I was six; he was fifty-one.

I thought of my Grandma Dulaney, who sewed a strap to a Martha White Self-Rising Flour sack so I could join my parents and aunts and uncles picking cotton. I sat on my Grandpa Dulaney's long sack as we all joined in a now dead southern tradition of families coming together at fall harvest to gather crops. I remember the hot red dirt coughing up little clouds of dust as Grandpa's sack scooted and paused up and down the dry rows of his modest patch of cotton and how the sharp husks pricked my fingers as I tried to pull the fluffy white bolls.

Sitting in the Capitol, I remembered my early days in the Mississippi hill counties of Itawamba and Tishomingo, both named after Chickasaw Indian Chiefs. These two Northeast Mississippi counties are located at the tag-end of the Appalachian Mountains. In the '50s and '60s, most Northeast Mississippi counties were just beginning to emerge from the traditions and ways of small family-owned subsistence farms to a world built around factories. My parents were part of the first generation of Mississippians to leave the farm and enter the factories. The plants, as we called them, were small garment operations lured to the South by promises of a loyal work force willing to work for low wages. My daddy worked for the Charm Step Shoe Company, which had plants in Itawamba and Tishomingo Counties. In my childhood we moved from Fulton to Iuka and back to Fulton as labor demands between the two plants dictated.

Because of our hops and skips around northeast Mississippi, I developed an early sense of loss that has in many ways become a part of who I am. I would give much of what I own today to have that little wooden wagon back. I still harbor some hope that one day I will find my little cotton sack. And I often wonder what became of many of my childhood friends in Tishomingo and Iuka.

Good school teachers made a big difference as I tried to catch up with each new class I joined, sometimes in the middle of a semester. Many stand out in my mind. I recall Miss Mamie Clarke of Iuka, who loved to read to her fourth graders about the adventures of Penrod, her voice rising and falling in tune with Penrod's heroics and misadventures. There was Beverly Jourdan, a beautiful young first year teacher who took my breath away in the fifth grade. I remember Miss Short in Tishomingo, who was tall. Miss Ruby Comer taught her Fulton sixth graders to diagram sentences with such ditties as "objects of preposition are never subjects of sentences" which the unlucky student sang solo when he committed such an error while diagramming a sentence on the blackboard. And there was the young Carolyn Hopkins, who taught seventh grade English in Fulton. Miss Hopkins loaned me college books to read outside of class and encouraged an early interest in law and politics.

All my childhood school teachers were women. In those days, school teaching was the highest calling available to most females. Women had not yet entered, in meaningful numbers, into other professions such as law or medicine or business. Today many of these ladies might not be found in the classroom. Rather, they are senior partners in law firms or bank presidents or maybe practicing medicine.

These are some of the folks who passed through my mind when Grady asked his question. I gave them all serious thought. Finally, I replied, "Well, Mr. President, I guess the person who has had the biggest positive influence in my life, up to this point, would have to be a woman.

He grinned impishly, implying a certain brotherhood.

"Was she good lookin'?"
"Well, yes," I said.
"A blonde?"
"No. Brunette."
"First love?"
"Um, not really."
"How old were you, eighteen?"
"Twelve."
"Twelve? My goodness." He looked at me in a new light. "What was her name?"
"Eupal Thornberry."
"Eupal?"
"Yes. My eighth grade English teacher. The finest English teacher in Mississippi. Miss Thornberry, as we called her, drilled us in the basic rules of grammar and spelling. I'll never forget "I before E, except after C." Miss Thornberry was a great English teacher. She was also the Bear Bryant of Itawamba County Spelling Bee coaches."

I explained to Grady that early in the eighth grade, Miss Thornberry determined that I had potential as a "speller." Spelling was a big deal in Itawamba County when I was growing up. Kids too small to play sports, like me in the eighth grade, or who lacked the necessary study habits, like me, to be scholars, could shine for a moment in the annual Itawamba County Spelling Bee. The Bee featured the best spellers from every Junior High and Grammar School in the county. Fulton, Fairview, Houston, Tremont, Mantachie and Dorsey.

Preparation for the Spelling Bee went on year-round. The sparring coaches and contestants practiced daily to earn the title of Itawamba County Spelling Bee Champion. Rewards for the Champion were many. The winner made the front page of our weekly newspaper, Delmus Harden's *Itawamba County Times,* whose motto was "The Only Newspaper in the World That Cares Anything About Itawamba County." The winning speller and coach would then compete in Memphis for the Mid-South Championship, sponsored by the old Memphis *Press-Scimitar* newspaper, and if you won there, go on to Washington, D.C., to spell for the National Championship. Spelling was big stuff in Itawamba County.

Miss Thornberry had won the county championship every year for more than two decades before I came along. She did it by hard work and discipline. She had even won the Mid-South Championship once, triumphing with the legendary Itawamba County speller, Wayne Thrash. Wayne took her all the way to Washington. Their hero status in Fulton nearly matched that of some of our best high school football players. Miss Thornberry now had high hopes for me. Tradition!

Well, Miss Thornberry and I won the Itawamba County Spelling Bee. This meant I stayed after school with Miss Thornberry every afternoon for several more weeks, preparing for the Memphis competition. She had quite a list of words for me to learn. Miss Thornberry didn't limit our practices to English words.

She was particularly fond of French words, springing such jewels as *tableaux* and *cabriolet* and *savoir-faire* on me.

In 1969 I was a short little fellow, sensitive about my height and painfully aware of my social awkwardness. All the girls in school were at least a head taller than me. I was too small to play football or basketball and wasn't particularly gifted in the classroom. Since my family had moved frequently from Fulton to Tishomingo to Iuka and back to Fulton during my grammar school years, I was a bit behind the other kids in junior high social relationships, so I didn't get invited to many parties. I was shy too. Over the years, books had become my best friends. Reading a good book, for me, has always been much like talking with a witty, well-educated conversationalist. Say, a Grady Tollison. Admittedly, all the talk may be one-sided if the writer is a good deal smarter than you. But isn't that how we learn? Read good books and you will grow, my friend.

My reading habits, inspired by my fine public school teachers, turned me into a county-level spelling savant. A prodigy of sorts. If I had ever seen a word, I could spell it. Might not know how to pronounce it (usually didn't) or what it meant. But I could spell it. Why? Because, in my wide, undisciplined reading of young George Washington; of Baron Munchausen; of Marvel comic books; of Sears-Roebuck catalogues; of the Bible; I had SEEN thousands of words. Not knowing any better, I pronounced the words in my mind as I saw them.

Antique became "anty-Q," and Bolshevik became "Bowl-she-vick," and so on. When the word antique, with the silent "ue" was called out to me in competition, my mind's eye clicked like a camera shutter and I saw the word, as though it were thrown on a screen. I would silently say to myself, "Well, that's how you pronounce 'anty-Q,'" and then confidently spell A-N-T-I-Q-U-E. Each spelled word was a small victory in one little boy's march toward self-confidence.

Miss Thornberry would bring fudge she had cooked at home or she would have the cafeteria cooks save us some "tater tots" for after-school snacks before we began our practice. She would grade papers at her desk as I had my snack. After these matters were finished, she would began calling out words. Our routine would go something like this:

Reconnaissance
R-E-C-O-N-N-A-I-S-S-A-N-C-E.
Catafalque
C-A-T-A-F-A-L-Q-U-E.
Sacroiliac
S-A-C-R-O-I-L-I-A-C.

Each afternoon we soon fell into a comfortable rhythm of words called and letters spelled back. My vocabulary and spelling skills expanded by the minute. But I was learning more than just words.

Miss Eupal Thornberry was teaching me self-discipline. To keep a clear head. She was teaching me to set

I'm Gonna Be A Diamond Some Day

Miss Eupal Thornberry and her speller

goals and to work hard. The time she spent with me had effects far beyond my obvious gains in spelling, vocabulary and learning the virtues of hard work. I sensed that if someone important and successful like her, someone in my estimation then, and now, who was the best in her field, could have an interest, and care about, someone little, like me, then there might be a chance for me too some day. She was teaching me that I had a chance in life. James Boswell says that Samuel Johnson said that his reading teacher, Donna Oliver, said that "he was the best scholar she had ever had," and that the venerable Johnson delighted in repeating her compliment, "adding, with a smile, that, 'this was as high a proof of his merit as he could conceive.'" I feel the same way about Miss Eupal Thornberry.

I shared my story of Miss Thornberry with Grady Tollison that afternoon in the Capitol. I told him that the moment I realized that I might be something some day came one afternoon as Miss Thornberry sat calling words and I sat spelling the words back to her, like a little Singer sewing machine making production. I was rolling. After an hour and a half, I had yet to mis-spell a single word. Then a life-changing event occurred. Miss Thornberry closed the speller, laid it on her desk, looked me in the eye, smiled kindly, and said to the little boy sitting across from her these simple words:

I believe you're the best I have ever had.

Wow! That moment, I told Grady Tollison, was when I knew there might be a place for me in life. My eighth grade English teacher had given me confidence. To quote one of her favorite poets, "And that has made all the difference."

I expected Tollison to tear up as I told my little story. Perhaps he might give me a brotherly (or, considering his age, fatherly) hug. We could wallow a few moments in good feeling. I waited. It didn't happen. He just sat there. Finally I asked, "Well, what do you think?"

He refused to be baited.

The jaded rascal grinned and said, "Well, Mr. Chairman, that's a really nice story. But the important question is: Have you had a woman tell you that *since*?"

Preachin', Prayin' and Politickin'

Let's talk about lawmakers and the Lord. Don't it make you proud to see folks in government pass laws, resolutions, rules and regulations promising to "put prayer back in the public schools." As though prayers weren't allowed? And don't you really want to holler Hally-loo-yah! when candidates for every office from constable to governor pledge to "put the Ten Commandments back" in the Capitol or the Courthouse or the health department or whatever public edifice they hope to inhabit? Outbreaks of piety and patriotism among the governing class typically occur about twelve months before an election. After all the fussing and cussing and voting are over, these issues will lie dormant for another three years or so until some new rabble-rouser catches an early case of campaign jitters and here we go again. Sometimes I am eager to hear certain candidates speak out on such issues. Otherwise, I wouldn't know where they stand.

While I respect, and will defend, the right of anyone to demagogue on issues of faith and state, it seems to me that these squabbles generally stir up more controversy than fellowship.

Let's look at the issue of public prayer. I admit I haven't read as much of the Bible as I should. (Nor as much as I intend to, Lord willing.) And I generally defer to our learned ecclesiastical authorities and TV preachers on the issue of when someone should utter a public prayer and who should have to listen to it. But I personally have trouble resolving the Sixth Chapter of Matthew with those seeking state-sponsored prayer. If we can accept Matthew as a reliable authority, Jesus told His followers, just before teaching them the Lord's Prayer:

> *And when thou prayest, thou shalt not be as the hypocrites are: for they love to pray standing in the synagogues and in the corners of the streets that they may be seen of men. Verily I say unto you, they have their reward.*

(Whoops! What about those public prayers at football games and NASCAR races? Is that the same as praying in the streets? I guess not.)

> *But thou, when thou prayest, enter into thy closet, and when thou hast shut thy door, pray to thy Father which is in secret and thy Father which seeth in secret shall reward thee openly.*

Now I won't go so far as to say that I have ever heard a hypocritical prayer at any public place, like a highway dedication or a football game. But I have heard some that were mighty long. And I submit there is a big difference between a football stadium and a closet. Do you think perhaps we sometimes confuse custom, habit and tradition with faith?

Now don't take me wrong. Little harm is done by public prayer anywhere. Even in a football stadium. And some good may come of it. But all things need to be put in perspective. I have my limits. I draw the line at playing football in a sanctuary.

I am also a bit wary of politicians in the pulpit and preachers running for public office. I have seen one or two in each category who have gone to the penitentiary. (The Lord does sometimes work in mysterious ways.)

I guess my philosophy is best expressed by the old Ecclesiastical pessimist who said that there is a time and place for everything. There is a time for preachin' and prayin' and a time for politickin'. But I think both faith and public policy suffer when the two are mixed. I sincerely believe that true faith is diminished when politicians begin touting religious matters. I just don't trust 'em. And I wish I could say that I have always felt that way. But I know better. I gained insight into the dangers of mixing politics and religion the old-fashioned way. I earned it in a figurative baptism of fire in 1983 when I first ran for a seat in the Mississippi Legislature.

I graduated from law school in 1980. Mona and Alysson and I moved to that beautiful old Queen City of the Tombigbee, Aberdeen, to join Bob and Jan Patterson's law firm. My first day on the job, they gave me a legal pad, a pen and a Dicta-Phone. Bob was always up on the latest technology and had invested a small fortune in Lanier word processors and dictation equipment. The dictation equipment absolutely fascinated me. I could pick up a telephone anywhere in the nation and call in to our central number and simply dictate away. Or I could shut the door to my office, pick up my portable Dicta-Phone, and just chat away. I could dictate driving down the road. I could dictate in a closet if I wished. Come to think of it, dictation is much like praying. You can even do it with your eyes closed. And you probably do a better job of it in private.

For the first two or three years of my law practice I spent many hours alone in my office, working on oil and gas drilling opinions, just dictating away. Sometimes it would be a day or two before a secretary got to my dictation, but my little letters or deeds or wills or drilling opinions would eventually come back, usually perfect. Much like answered prayers.

My first secretary was a wonderful lady, Emily Blankenship, now Seymer. After my first rather clumsy efforts at dictation, Emily came into my office one morning and asked if she could suggest some improvements in my technique. She was professional about the matter and careful not to make me feel too wet behind the ears. Emily knew there were some things a young lawyer needed to know which he never learned in law school but that he might be sensitive about learning from a secretary. (Another lesson in life. Learn from everyone.)

Emily first suggested that I punctuate my sentences as I dictated: at the end of a sentence, to say "period;" to say "comma" when one needed to be inserted; and to say "paragraph" when I wanted a new one to begin. She said such instructions would make her job much easier. Then she brought up another matter.

Emily said that it didn't look very professional for me to write a demand letter, threatening to sue someone, and close that letter with the common phrases "Fondly" or "Best Wishes." She suggested that legal correspondence needed a certain formality and dignity.

I blushed a little and told her that I certainly agreed.

She waited a few moments, not saying anything, in that polite way she had of trying to make me think that things were my idea. I fell for it as usual and finally asked if she had any suggestions on improving my letter closings. Not to my surprise, she said she did. She told me that her previous boss, Russ Grant, always ended his letters with a flourish, as follows:

> *With kindest personal regards,*
> *I remain,*
> *Sincerely yours,*

I told her that would be fine with me and thanked her

for educating me in proper legal etiquette. We had no more problems, as far as I know, with my dictation.

Thereafter, I spent hundreds of happy hours in my little office, dictating away, sometimes with my eyes closed. And I would end every letter as follows:

> *With kindest personal regards,*
> *I remain,*
> *Sincerely yours,*
> *Michael P. Mills*

I began to take a little pride at seeing my name at the end of the well-typed letters springing from Emily's typewriter like answers to prayers, always graced in closing with that wonderful professional rhetorical flourish,

> *With kindest personal regards,*
> *I remain,*
> *Sincerely yours,*
> *Michael P. Mills*

(Michael Paul. I was named after an angel and an apostle. My friends and family know that I am neither.)

After a time, I got involved in politics and ran for the office of District 21 of the Mississippi House of Representatives.

When a fellow gets in politics, he finds out soon enough that an awful lot of folks want to advise him on what he should do. Weekdays are busy as one tries to balance a fairly normal personal life and the usual job responsibilities with politics. But weekends are frantic. The politician gets invited to chicken fights, quilting bees, stock car races, Little League baseball games and dozens of county speakin's, and more garden clubs and civic organizations than you can shake a limp dishrag at. And, of course, a good politician can't miss Sunday church services. I've noticed that church attendance really picks up just before an election. But church folk tend to be gracious and forgiving, so not much is said, at least in church, about candidates' election eve attendance. Since I had become a politician and needed to be seen in public as often as possible, I didn't miss many events and carried myself fairly well . . . until I started mixing politics and religion.

One of my supporters called to say that her little country church was having a cemetery Decoration Day on Saturday and she thought I really should attend. I thanked her for calling but questioned whether it would be proper for me to make a political appearance at a church. (I wasn't sure my friends from Sandy Springs and East Fulton would understand this business of mixing politics and religion.) She assured me that this would be no problem and hinted that I might receive some special recognition for my attendance. I thanked her again but said "I just don't think that would look right." She then mentioned that she *thought* one of my opponents would probably attend since "He has kinfolk buried there." Well! Say howdy!

I thanked her for inviting me, said "I would *probably* be there," and stewed the remainder of the week over whether I should attend this service. She was a dear old saint from out near the Bigbee community, and I didn't want to disappoint her. On the other hand I didn't wish to be thought of . . . well . . . you know . . . as hypocritical. It had not occurred to me at this point that hypocrisy is a twin to demagoguery. I couldn't make up my mind.

Saturday morning arrived and my competitive instincts got the better of discretion and good taste and I decided I should go. I put on my best pinstriped suit, the one with a vest, and a starched white shirt and my black wing tips and headed out into the country, resolved to conduct myself with as much dignity as possible during the Decoration Day ceremonies. And, I must admit, I was looking forward to maybe receiving a little favorable recognition for my attendance. And besides, if one of my opponents was there, I wouldn't look too out of place. On the other hand if he wasn't there, even better!

The little white country church, with its modest steeple, seemed to glow from a distance as I drove down the dusty gravel road. I was an early arrival and noticed immediately that the other folks were dressed fairly casually for a religious service. Most of the men had on short-sleeved shirts and work boots. Only the preacher had on a tie. Someone handed me a hoe.

I enthusiastically joined the work and soon shed my coat. I rounded up graves and tossed armfuls of last year's plastic flowers over the fence and otherwise contributed as best I could to the community efforts. After a couple of hours, and several glasses of ice water poured from gallon jugs, we heard voices drifting from the open windows of the old church house. "Oh come, come, come, come. . . . Come to the church in the valley. . . ." I joined the other members of the work gang, and meandered toward the church, wiping red dusty sweat from my brow with the sleeve of my starched white shirt.

I hoped that we would hear a short homily from the preacher, and thought possibly that he might say something about the nice young lawyer running for the legislature being there, and I could half stand and modestly bow toward the congregation and give them a gentle half wave of my hand and smile timidly, as though I didn't deserve the recognition, and then quietly sit down and later, after the service maybe, shake their hands and thank them for inviting me and never say a word about politics. I would win them with my modesty and good taste of not politicking on church grounds! Well, I was mistaken.

No short homily for this preacher. He gave us the full 45-minute dose. I am embarrassed to say that I can't recall the subject of his sermon, but his style included a lot of grunting. I remember that by the end of this sermon, I had resorted to counting dirt daubers flying in and out of the windows. I also became aware of the sweaty red dust inching its way between my neck and the starched collar of my tightly buttoned shirt. I was getting really itchy when finally the tone of the sermon slowed and he began his wind-down. I perked up and suspected he might be ready to shut it down and possibly might say something pleasant about me, when he said, to my disappointment, "And now, I'll introduce Brother Moak, who has a few words to say." "Well, my goodness," I thought, but kept my feelings to myself.

Brother Moak preached a while with even more gusto than his predecessor. I am sure preachers don't fall into this trap, since they are only delivering to the sheep the message the Good Lord lays on 'em, but I can't help comparing one to another when they preach back to back. And the second preacher was definitely louder than the old, white-haired father he had followed. He spoke on the subject of sin, and, I took it, was generally against it. Despite the volume, however, I started getting a little bit heat-drowsy. I became hypnotized by the gentle action of the slowly turning ceiling fans and wondered how the dirt daubers kept from bouncing off the blades. It was also dawning on me that with two preachers in the house it was very unlikely that a politician would get any recognition whatsoever. I was resigned to my fate and hoped I wouldn't fall asleep before the sermon ended. It had gone on for about 30 more minutes when Brother Moak's tenor changed and it became apparent that his sermon was about to be wrapped up. I relaxed as he ended his message and also took a seat behind the pulpit. The old preacher then rose and said, "And now we have another speaker today." My ears perked up!

Surely I wasn't going to be invited into the pulpit! On second thought, maybe I would be asked to say a few words. But no, he introduced a visiting preacher from over in Alabama, who then got up and blessed us with another message. Sad to say, I don't recall his subject either.

Well, you can imagine how I felt getting my third sermon of the day, sitting in a hot, black suit, sweat-streaked and dusty after having spent two hours hoeing in the cemetery. However, I am an optimist by nature, and made the best of the situation by trying to surreptitiously count the number of pine planks in the ceiling. I fancied I even had an angelic look as I glanced toward the ceiling listening to the third message. Well, soon enough, the Alabama preacher started winding down and again everyone seemed to relax. He took his seat and the first old preacher called for the invitation and another old brother stood up and started leading the assemblage in one of my favorite old standards and I easily slipped into the gentle rhythm and voice of the congregation. ". . . Just as I am . . . without one plea . . . but that Thy blood . . . was shed for me. . . ."

I noticed the women rising and politely easing out of the sanctuary as the invitation continued. Women in country churches have an advantage in times like these. They don't have to wait through the entire invitation because they have to get busy setting the table for dinner on the grounds. I could just see the tops of their heads through the windows as they busied themselves covering the long wooden table which ran alongside the church with white butcher paper and could hear the tinkle of china as they set bowls and silverware and plates on the table. My mind started wandering again and I had visions of wonderful cold fried chicken, home-cooked rolls, sweet tea and all the wonderful condiments that go with a country church dinner on the grounds. My favorite delicacy at such occasions is deviled eggs. I never get deviled eggs at home. The only place I ever eat deviled eggs is at church. I have thought about that a lot. Why do we eat deviled eggs at church? Well, I was lazily toying with this important question when the invitation finally ended and the preacher made an astounding request. Remember I had hoped at some time during the service that he or one of the other preachers, or perhaps one of the women in charge of keeping the cemetery clean, would say something like "We're glad to have young Mike Mills visiting with us today." And I would be able to stand and modestly wave and sit back down having accomplished my mission. Well, a sermon or two earlier, I had given up hope. Now, I just wanted to get to the dinner table as soon as possible. Maybe they would have the sweet tea already poured. I wasn't prepared for what happened next.

When the invitation ended, the preacher stood up and in his wonderful *basso profundo* said with a sweet broad-faced smile, "And now Brother Mills will lead us in closing prayer." I was stunned! It occurred to me, exactly at that moment, that I had never prayed in public. He may as well have asked me to sing the national anthem! Now don't get me wrong, I have had plenty of opportunities in life to pray. But since the subjects of my prayer were often so deeply personal, I had never felt moved to voice any of my prayers in public. I much preferred a closet. I had never prayed out loud, even in Sunday School, where one is supposed to learn such things. Probably, none of my Sunday school teachers had ever suspected me of being a suspect for a good public prayer. So I had made it thus far in life without praying in public. That's a real problem when you're a young politician and want to make a good show at everything you do.

Different churches have different ways of praying. If I had been in an Episcopal church, I could have just grabbed a Book of Common Prayer, opened it on about any page, and read a good prayer. That's one of the good things about Episcopalians. Most of them are literate and always have access to good prayers. Likewise, had I had been in a Pentecostal church, a faith for which I have great respect and affection, I would not have been on the spot. In Pentecostal services, everybody prays at the same time. We would have all stood up and prayed as we pleased and I wouldn't have had to worry about getting it right. No one would be able to compare my prayer to anyone else's because we would all be praying together. And had it been a Methodist church, I could probably have gotten by without worrying about any particular phrases. Methodists are wonderfully tolerant folks. However, this was an old country Baptist church and I knew that there was a certain way to do it right. Good country prayers have to have certain phrases in them or they don't ring true. I knew that much because I had heard a bunch of 'em growing up. Unfortunately, at that exact moment, I couldn't recall any of those phrases. I was in a bind. And besides the phrases, should I kneel or stand up? Different churches do it differently. I kind of looked around and noticed that everyone had their heads bowed and were standing so I thought it would be okay to stand and I just shut my eyes and waited for inspiration or lightning to strike. Either would have been appreciated.

Some people are good cussers and some are good prayers. Those who are good at both know that brevity enhances delivery. There is an art to rendering a good public prayer. I also knew from trying cases and giving political speeches that one should have a definite subject in mind before making any public utterances. An outline is usually helpful. The same rules apply to good public praying. Unfortunately, I didn't have time to make any notes.

Right after Jesus told us how to pray, as in go to a closet, he commenced The Lord's Prayer, which begins "Our Father, Who art in Heaven. . . ." It's still a pretty good model to follow. So that's how I started my prayer. It has a nice ring to it and really got me going. Well, after I got through the "Our Father Who Art in Heaven" part, I started trying to think of something that would be particularly appropriate to pray about in front of all these folks. This church had many older men from that special generation who fought in World War II. Patriotism is always popular so, in my panic to grasp something appropriate to pray about, I started praying for the sailors overseas. I had no sooner got that out of my mouth than I realized that many of the local Tombigbee area servicemen had served in forces other than the Navy, and, being a politician, I didn't want to leave anybody out so I prayed for the Air Force and for the Army, too. But something was wrong here. Having a diplomatic mind, I wanted to include all branches of the U.S. Armed Services and I knew that there were four branches. But at this particular moment I couldn't think of the fourth branch. My mind was racing faster than a U-2 jet and I heard myself mumbling something about the Seabee's. This didn't sound quite right but I did get a fourth branch in there anyway and was desperately wracking my brain for something else to pray about when a term I have heard in an awful lot of good country prayers came to my mouth and I started praying for the "sick and the afflicted." I even named a couple in the church who I thought needed particular attention and then I started worrying that I may have offended them or perhaps someone else would be offended whom I didn't name.

Well, I staggered through the sick and afflicted . . . the infirm . . . the shut-ins . . . and the mentally ill . . . anxiously grasping for something else to pray about and then remembered several good old country prayers I had heard in the past that dealt with jail house ministries. So I started praying for the people in jail, too.

These were all worthy topics for a good ole timey country prayer, but I simply wasn't satisfied with my performance. All of this sounded rather hollow to me. I feared it rang rather amateurish to my listeners. My first public prayer wasn't going too well. I felt inadequate since I couldn't ring those magical phrases and words which must be said in a good country prayer. That's when the Marines jumped into my mind and I mentally back-pedaled and started praying for the sailors overseas again and worked myself through the Air Force and then the Army and grandly asked for His blessings upon the Marines.

About this time, the old preacher went "hrumph" real loud, because I was on his time now. He startled me. I realized I was taking a little too long. Food was getting cold. When the preacher said "hrumph," those missing magical phrases dropped before my mind like manna from Heaven! My confidence soared! My volume increased! I was ready to wind this matter up in grand provincial fashion.

I swelled up big deep inside and in my best country fashion voiced those magic country Baptist words, asking the Good Lord to "Bless the hands that prepared this food, and bless this food to the nourishment of our bodies and our bodies to Thy service." Boy, did I feel good to get that out!

I was on a roll. I had the hang of it. So I went back and started praying for the people in the jails and hospitals and toyed with the sick and afflicted. But doubt again crept into my mind. I didn't know how to turn it off. Have you ever thought about that? How would you tell a person to end a prayer? I needed Miss Emily to finish her lecture. I couldn't stop. Well, I wandered around in my prayer, expanding its scope and vision, and started yet again on the Armed Services when the preacher said for the second time, "Hrumph!" A little louder this time. That's when I panicked! It was just like dictating. The preacher had startled me and I knew my end was coming, like it or not. Undoubtedly the ice was melting in the tea glasses, the fried chicken was getting dry, and the cornbread was going stale. I had to shut this thing down. That's when I heard those magic words leap from my mouth as I closed my first public prayer:

With kindest personal regards,
I remain,
Sincerely yours,
Michael P. Mills.

The Three Kings of Tombigbee Country

In 1980, the good folks of Aberdeen welcomed me into their community about as warmly as a young lawyer can be invited into peaceful environs. Soon enough I began to learn (at the expense of my clients) all the things they don't teach in law school about the practice of law. I received my instructions in trial court advocacy firsthand from the not always gentle, but without fail, honorable, lectures and closing arguments and vigorous cross-examinations (of clients, not me) of Dave Houston and Dick Booth and other leading lights of the Monroe County Bar. After two or three years of such seasoning, I decided to add some variety to my life and run for the Mississippi Legislature.

I confess that I didn't have a lot of encouragement to seek public office. In fact, I suspect many folks were surprised to hear that I had thrown my hat in the ring. Unlike Cincinnatus of ancient times, I had no coalition of business folk or lawyers or school teachers or anybody else actively urging me to run. No newspaper editorials called for my candidacy. No cadre of concerned citizens knocked on my door. (Though Dick Booth, in his polite, courtly manner seemed to favor my candidacy. I guess he saw my election as a good way to get me out of town for three or four months of the year.) But, with or without a public outcry, I jumped into the race by paying $15 at the Circuit Clerk's office.

Many friends contributed time and advice. Eden Martin of Prairie served as my campaign Chairman and was the real brains behind my election. A poet named Sam Prestridge, who lived in an abandoned beauty shop outside Smithville, came out of the woods and wrote brilliant jingles and slogans for radio spots and newspaper ads. Others volunteered to put up yard signs and such. We had tons of energy and some goodwill in the community. Our prospects looked good.

Sam and Eden decided that I had to run as "More Than Just Another Politician." I was a little uncomfortable with that slogan, since, having paid $15 to run, I *was* a politician. But the slogan had a nice ring. And so we went with it. Today, it's popular for candidates for public office to say, "I'm not a politician." Don't let 'em fool you. That is like a fellow in a white gown about to do surgery in the emergency room stating "I'm not a doctor." The point I'm trying to make is that when you pay your money to run for public office, you become a politician. And so did I.

District 21, the seat I was seeking, included all of Aberdeen and roughly the west half of Monroe County and the southern one-third of Itawamba County. The district is a wonderful microcosm of Mississippi. It is divided by the straight levees of the Tennessee-Tombigbee Waterway and seasoned with the meanderings of the old Tombigbee River. The northern part of District 21 is "hill" country" while the southern half of the district, the prairie area in particular, has more of an Old South plantation mystique. This district mirrored the entire state with its diverse mixture of flatlanders and hill people, black folk and white folk, and merchants and wage-earners and country squires. I gained insights in 1983 into how much we are all alike, rather than how we differ. And I learned that we're shaped not only by blood but by place. My psychic sense of place will always rest in Monroe and Itawamba.

My campaign committee didn't have much money to spend on advertising, and we couldn't afford a huge staff. So the gang put me on the road. In addition to praying in churches, I also did what any energetic candidate does the first time he or she seeks public office: I went *door-to-door*.

Going door -to- door works only once. The old adage, "there ain't nothin' like the first time" certainly applies in politics. The people are invariably tolerant and kind to a fresh prospect. They will give you a lot of sweet tea and sympathetic encouragement. But the second time around, look out! The second time you go door-to-door, folks greet you with, "Well, it's about time you came by. We ain't seen you in four years" and, "Boy, have I been waiting on you to come back around. . . . I've got a bone to pick with you on how you voted on . . ." And so on.

After one's first term in office, the veteran learns to stage public appearances at places like libraries and public schools and other public places where few people will show up, but the newspapers will give you good coverage.

Going door-to-door, I learned much about the traits, customs and beliefs of folks in the Tombigbee River counties. The graciousness I received in the dining rooms and on the front porches of the voters in Aberdeen and Nettleton, Wren and Bounds Cross Roads, Tremont and Dorsey and so many other Northeast Mississippi communities will stay with me forever. I learned how to give a pretty good stump speech and rediscovered my forgotten talent for shelling purple-hull peas. The pitfalls and disasters I sidestepped or muddled through in my first political race were invaluable growth opportunities. For instance, what would you do if an addled old parson began appearing at crossroads speakings in opposition to your candidacy, handing out crude brochures attacking you personally with the following doggerel:

Vote against whiskey,
Vote against stills.
Vote against Catholics,
Vote against Mills.

While this poem has a certain catchy ring, it is basically untrue. I am not a Catholic, though I admire many traditions in the Catholic faith. However, rather than allow this to become a campaign issue by publicly denying that I was a Catholic, I simply made sure every Catholic in District 21 got a copy of the brochure.

More important, I learned that folks are about the same wherever one goes. Human nature is constant. Everyone wants to believe in something bigger than himself. And what we believe in has as much to do with where we're from as who we are. We are products of place as much as chance. Nothing illustrates these lessons better than the Three Kings of Tombigbee Country whom I discovered in 1983.

I found the first king in the homes of my favorite voters, the kindly old folks living on dusty gravel roads out in the country. These people often struggled to survive on small Social Security checks supplemented by a neat truck patch behind the house. Their lives revolved around church and gardening and attending RCDC meetings. Most of them, like my grandparents, came of age during the Great Depression. They never enjoyed many advantages in life, yet they managed to find many small joys. In times of crisis, they're the first to offer help, though they often have the least to give. They are special. And in my door-to-door efforts, I often sat on the old folks' porches and drank their tea and shelled a few bowls of peas now and then and generally just let them charm me with their simple, honest outlook on life. They were always "glad for comp'ny," even if it was a politician. And in their humble homes I learned that what we have . . . what we honor . . . reflects who we are.

One symbol of the old folk's sense of identity stands out in my mind more than the all the other bric-a-brac and doo-dads and what-nots I saw in their homes. A majority of the Depression era folk had one particular icon hanging in their homes that represents their world view as well as anything I know. Nearly always, somewhere in the house, the old man or the old woman or the old couple would have a certain picture hanging on the wall. The print would be surrounded by a plastic frame, sometimes illumined by a hooded lightbulb. One could pull a little chain attached to the light fixture and cast a golden glow upon a painting of Jesus standing at a door, knocking.

Invariably, I would ask about the picture. I always received the same gentle explanation. That the door Jesus was knocking on has no handle. The old lady or the old man would then tell me that the door represented my heart and that the only way Jesus could enter my heart was from within. I had to open the door. Over two decades later, this picture of Jesus knocking at the door remains in my mind, reminding me of the humble country folks who gave me not only their votes, but much more in 1983. They taught me to respect the virtue of humility.

I found the second king in the homes and churches and stores of African-Americans. My momma raised me to respect all persons equally, without regard to race, religion, color or creed. And she felt that way well before the civil rights movement. In 1983, we Mississippians were still learning to live and work together as diverse peoples. (The same is true throughout America even today.) Of course, our diversity affected our politics. Some politicians were afraid to go door-to-door in black neighborhoods and some were afraid to go into "rich folks" neighborhoods and some were afraid to go anywhere. My political instincts (and the law) told me that all votes counted the same. And I wanted every vote. I hoped for a unanimous election, if possible.

I gladly knocked on doors in African-American neighborhoods, and I visited in black churches, when invited. Again, I made many friends, sitting on porches or speaking from pulpits, and yes, shelling a few bowls of peas. African-Americans have special icons too. In their homes and churches one may also find a picture of Jesus knocking at the door. But they had another talisman still to be found in small cafes and certain road houses and blues clubs and in black homes throughout Mississippi. Somewhere in the house, usually in the kitchen, or perhaps in the small den, one will find an old green cardboard church fan with a wooden handle, or perhaps a dinner plate, or maybe a framed picture hanging from the wall, depicting Martin Luther King, Jr., flanked by President John F. Kennedy and his late brother Robert. Dead martyrs to a living cause.

There is one more King in our Tombigbee counties. Senior citizens and African-Americans weren't the only voters in my district. I also visited in the house trailers and small FHA homes and crowded apartments of working class citizens. From them, I found other icons representative of who we are as a people. I soon learned to predict with reasonable certainty which small home would have a picture of Elvis Presley hanging somewhere in the house. In the 1980's, Elvis, though dead, was still the King in the hearts and minds of many hard-working folks in Monroe and Itawamba Counties. He was sometimes pictured in a sequined suit kicking a painful-looking karate chop; sometimes leaning forward into a microphone with his guitar strapped to his back, his heels pointed in opposite directions, his knees bent and a wild look on his face; sometimes in just a handsome close-up portrait. The King of Rock-N-Roll may have replaced some other Kings in our collective consciousness. We are what we honor.

Well, the folks who supported the Three Kings supported me, (though not unanimously), and I got elected to the Legislature where I served for twelve years.

A few years ago, while I was still practicing law, I had a client visiting from out of state. We finished our court work and as I drove him to Tupelo to catch his plane, he mentioned that he had always been a fan of Elvis Presley and that he understood that Elvis' birthplace was in Tupelo. He asked if we had time to visit. I said, "Sure, I've always wanted to go myself."

On the way I told him of the Three Kings of our Tombigbee Country: Elvis, Martin Luther King, Jr., and Jesus. I didn't know at the time, but my story was not yet complete.

Many of you have probably visited Elvis' birthplace in Tupelo. For fifty cents you can tour a very nice air-conditioned museum and view sequined jumpsuits; gold albums; a guitar or two; posters advertising Elvis's movies; and other paraphernalia dealing with the King's life and career. There is even a hammer hanging on the wall, with an affidavit attached, vouching that the hammer in question had been used by Elvis's daddy to build the shotgun house which was Elvis's birthplace. There is also a chapel on the grounds and a small monument to Elvis, where his fans often leave flowers and sometimes tape letters to the stone, pledging their undying love. Not unlike written prayers stuffed into a desert wailing wall.

The highlight of the grounds is the little shotgun house, built by the hammer on the wall, where Elvis was born. My client and I saved the little house for last. In keeping with the mood, we reverently entered. In the front room we found a small wood stove and some crude furniture and a doorway leading into a small kitchen with another doorway leading into a tiny room in the back which contained a small bed and a dresser. That's the entire house. And I probably wouldn't have remembered much had it not been for one other item we saw. Hanging on the wall in the front room of the birthplace of the King of Rock-N-Roll is a picture of Jesus . . . knocking at the door.

The Sun-N-Sand Years

Home Away From Home

A word about the Sun-N-Sand. I roomed at the downtown Jackson Sun-N-Sand Resort Motel for several legislative sessions. Located one block West of the Capitol, the Sun-N-Sand was home away from home for roughly one-half the House membership and one or two Senators. Practically all the Northeast Mississippi delegation roomed there. (Many Senators, sensitive to preserving their enviable status as members of the upper house, tended to rent more expansive quarters elsewhere.)

The Sun-N-Sand Resort Motel and Restaurant lacked sandy beaches, crashing waves or cute tiki bars, though it did have a pool which was heated in the summertime. The inside amenities, like many of us, were a bit common. The bedroom walls were paper thin and all units were heated and cooled by a central thermostat. The complimentary soap and plastic courtesy cups, furnished once a week, were surplus Holiday Inn supplies. And ambience! I waked each morning to the smell of stale cigarettes, courtesy of the community cooling and heating system. In their defense, the hotel management stubbornly battled this irritating problem. In the afternoons, our rooms smelled like oranges. Apparently the room service ladies were instructed to spray the rooms with some sort of tropical spray, consistent with the motel's sunny, beach-front resort theme. As a bonus, the spray masked not only the cigarette smoke, but also the funk rising from the 1950's era yellow shag carpet.

Taking a shower in a Sun-N-Sand bathroom was a real adventure. Alert bathing habits were some of the most important skills a young legislator could develop. First one learned to rise early for morning ablutions. Many of my fellows at the motel were, shall we say, country boys. They were early risers by nature. Consequently, by eight o'clock in the morning, most of the hot water was gone. I am a reasonably quick study. After two or three mornings of cold nine o'clock showers, I adapted to the country boys' ways. I became an early riser. I soon learned that the hottest water was available between 5:30 and 6:00 a.m. Which led to another growth opportunity.

The young solon showering in the Sun-N-Sand soon developed an acute sensitivity to water pressure. If a neighbor flushed his commode, the person showering suffered a near-scalding surprise as cold water was diverted from the shower head to other purposes. I learned to quickly dart out of the stream at the slightest quiver of shower head pressure. Once out of the shower, other challenges presented. Drying off became an art form itself. The thin white motel towels were nearly transparent and just barely wide enough to cover one's butt. We soon learned to stow a few towels between the mattresses and thereby get ahead of the cleaning ladies' cycles in order to have enough material to dry reasonably after a shower.

Most folks stayed at the Sun-N-Sand for one of two reasons. Either the low rates or the fellowship. I was there for both reasons. Despite our slipshod furnishings and paucity of luxuries, the Sun-N-Sand inmates developed a sophisticated social order not unlike that found in other societies.

The undisputed "Godfather" of the Sun-N-Sand was my Tombigbee Country neighbor from Union County, Representative John David Pennebaker. John David was Chairman of the House Transportation Committee and served as the hotel's unofficial dorm manager. His chief buddies were future House Speaker Billy McCoy, from downtown Rienzi and Mike Eakes, our "Big Indian" from Neshoba County. (These men later successfully led the fight, over Governor Allain's veto, to pass the 1987 Highway Reform Act. Most of the real work, including a good deal of the arm-twisting, leading to passage of this important legislation, happened after hours at the Sun–N-Sand.)

John David Pennebaker is a good Presbyterian, a fine lawyer, and a born aristocrat. He is well aware of his rightful place near the top of the social pecking order of life. John David insists on order and a certain dignified reticence in all one's personal and professional relationships. Though he lacked any actual authority, John David prevailed upon the motel managers to allow him to assign rooms. Hence the nickname "The Godfather." I guess it was predestined. One soon learned to stay in John David's good graces if you wanted a first floor room opening onto the pool. Otherwise he would put you upstairs overlooking the rear parking lot nearest the Farish Street gunfire.

I was assigned Room 108, right in line with The Godfather, Billy McCoy, the Big Indian and my old Delta friend, Jimmy Green, who was like a grandfather to me and who was also on the Transportation commit-

The "Godfather" John David Pennebaker, with a favored host, John Dennery and Robert Clark

tee. This hotel room line-up had a lot to do with the fact that my home town at the time, Aberdeen, got on the 1987 four-lane highway map. It was good to have friends at the Sun-N-Sand.

As time passed, the Godfather began deciding which receptions I would attend, which lobbyists would take me to dinner and what time I could call home each night. And Lordy, Lordy if anyone sneaked out without letting John David know where he was going and with whom.

Much of our Sun-N-Sand life spun around the big round table in the back of the restaurant where House members swapped gossip and yarns between servings of ham and bacon and hot biscuits delivered crisp and steaming by the delightful Miss Suzy. (I never knew Suzy's last name but I will never forget her cheerfully hopping from table to table, favoring one braced knee, always remembering with a smile who liked scrambled eggs and who wanted theirs sunny-side-up. She had served legislators and lobbyists and gubernatorial wannabes and junior college presidents and like ilk for more than forty years, stretching back to the days of the old King Edward Hotel. I consider her a great American. We later surprised her with a resolution in her honor and a standing ovation in the House of Representatives. After working only two blocks from the Capitol for forty years, this was the first time she had ever entered the building.)

Two Delta elites from the legislative class of 1960, Charlie Deaton and Sonny Merideth, often joined us at the Sun-N-Sand. Charlie and Sonny command attention in any assembly.

Charlie Deaton, from Greenwood, was reared an orphan and became a fine college football player at Millsaps. Today he is one of this State's most valued senior statesmen. Tall and slender, with his trademark silver hair and gray-blue eyes, Charlie's face breaks into a thousand crinkles of good-feeling when he smiles, which is often. He has aged well, giving one the sense of a smooth, well-oiled old blade of steel. Charlie enjoys good bird-hunts, good food and good conversation. If you can't cook or talk, Charlie will be glad to do both. He has served as Chairman of Appropriations in the House, a valued member of the State Board of Education and official and un-official adviser to a number of governors, including Winter, Allain, and Fordice. Charlie says of all the things he has done in life, he would like to be back in the Mississippi legislature just to see Sonny Merideth cry one more time.

Sonny Merideth, from Greenville, has classic good looks which are sometimes confounded by a subtle gray scowl. His alert hazel eyes and heavy dark brows give fair warning of his quick intelligence. My former colleague John Grisham immortalized Sonny in the character of Nathan Locke in his best-selling novel, *The Firm*. John describes Nathan Locke, the villain of the piece:

Mitch nodded and knew for certain he had never been within a hundred yards of Nathan

> *Locke. He would have remembered. It was the eyes, the cold black eyes with layers of black wrinkles around them. Great eyes. Unforgettable eyes. His hair was white and thin on top with thickets around the ears, and the whiteness contrasted sharply with the rest of his face. When he spoke, the eyes narrowed and the black pupils glowed fiercely. Sinister eyes. Knowing eyes. (62)*

John captures Sonny's dark side. There is another side to the man. Those same eyes moisten at the slightest hint of injustice. And his high clear tenor voice can touch every note of human experience.

Sonny was one of the great orators in State government. During my time in the House, Sonny, along with Jim Simpson, Sr., Billy McCoy of Rienzi and Ed Perry, the little giant from Oxford, could each move the House at will with brilliance and feeling. Simpson and Perry and McCoy could be great on any given day and on any given issue. But, as Charlie Deaton says, nobody can cry like Sonny. About once a session Sonny would get really worked up about an issue and after three or four days of floor fights, parliamentary back-stabbings and general hysteria among the membership about whatever might be the issue, Sonny would finally take the podium. He would first state the facts as he knew them. He would then qualify the facts that he did not know with the statement, "I am told but do not know . . ." and ramble on about the options and the merits on this side or the other, and so on until, having stated the facts and presented both sides, he came to his magic words: "search your hearts and search your minds," and you knew something good was coming then. The tears couldn't be far.

Sonny is ethical, honest and loyal to a fault. Like many strong-willed people, Sonny inspires deep feelings in others. Most members deeply admired his abilities. Some feared his intellect. A few, with less ability, were intensely jealous. He was respected by all. He first chaired Judiciary "A" and later the Ways and Means Committee under Speaker Buddy Newman. When the winds of change began to blow in the 1980's, Sonny was loyal to Newman to the end. He was demoted by the new regime to Chairman of County Affairs. He never whined and served ably and admirably in this position, writing and leading to passage the "County Unit" legislation which helped reform county government.

Sonny never traded votes, which means "I'll vote for your bill here, if you'll vote for my bill there." I understand this practice is known in Congress as "log rolling," and is there considered a highly specialized art. Sonny called it "linkage" and absolutely despised the practice. He thought every bill should stand on its own merits and every member should stand on his own abilities.

In my years with Sonny, he always paid his own way and made his own way. I never saw a lobbyist offer him a favor. I never saw him swap a vote. If he had a fault, it may have been that folk of lesser abilities thought he sometimes enjoyed the fight more than the victory.

Charlie and Sonny were big buddies with "Teddy" Millete, the Chairman of Public Health during my first four years in the House. Teddy grew up with Sonny in Greenville. He was also a veteran and, in college, was a brilliant running-back on the Ole Miss football team. Outside the legislature, he was a successful businessman. Teddy may be the sweetest man I ever knew. We still mourn his passing in the Fall of 2004.

I spent too much time in the Sun-N-Sand Bar with another service veteran, my friend Jim Simpson, Sr., from Harrison County. Jim was a big man with a big heart who spoke a rich coastal brogue. A very, very bright person, he knew more law than most lawyers. Jim was a strong supporter of public education and

Sonny Merideth cross-examines Mr. Jerry Wilburn

children's health issues. He often told me that "The people of Mississippi are braver than her leaders." I think he was right. Unlike many old timers in State government, Jim never feared change. He believed in the future. Our world would be much better today if he were still around. He also had a fine grasp of irony.

One benefit to legislative service is the joy of getting to know some fine folks from all over the State. Mississippi can be fairly divided into five regions, each with its own culture. There is the Delta, with its flat, rich soil and high African-American population. For years the Delta controlled politics in Mississippi, often at odds with my part of the state, once known as the "Poor Northeast Hill Counties." The Piney Woods region covers East Central Mississippi and borders the Capital region which consists of Jackson and surrounding counties. Finally, there is the Gulf Coast, which enjoys a diverse mix of people from all over the world. Some regions have a stronger identity than others, and it is a real test of legislative mettle for a member to vote for a program which may benefit another region when the folks back home are opposed to the program.

The Gulf Coast legislators had the strongest regional identity among the membership during my twelve years in the House, often caucusing in the Rules Committee room. Due to his long seniority in the House, and no doubt, due to his superior intellect, Jim Simpson, Sr. was the de facto leader of the Coast delegation and often had his hands full keeping this delegation in line. The caucus complicated life in the House for Jim since he considered himself a "State" Representative rather than a representative for only one county or region.

Curt Hebert, later to become a Public Service Commissioner and member of the Federal Energy Regulatory Commission, was a lively member of the Class of 1988 from Pascagoula. The studious and polite Danny Guice, from Ocean Springs, was another member of the Gulf Coast delegation.

The Rules Committee Room has a long, formal oak table surrounded by heavy stuffed chairs. These chairs are about the size and weight of a recliner. The Coast delegation met there regularly to discuss their regional interests. On one such occasion, Representative Hebert got into an argument with another member seated across the table. Their dispute became heated and personal insults were exchanged. Hebert, who is not a large man, but who is a former college football player, grabbed one of the chairs and slung it across the table at his adversary. He missed. Afterward, Jim Simpson, Sr. told me in his deep, baritone brogue, "However, the *effuht* was not *entahly* wasted. He *did* hit Danny Guice."

The Night Life, Ain't No Good Life . . .

Lawyers, bankers, doctors, used car dealers, school teachers, insurance agents, small businessmen, large businessmen, widget manufacturers, regulators of widget manufacturers and a few lonely housewives and other influence peddlers stalk members of the legislature like a chronic bad cold. These folks are commonly known as lobbyists, though most enjoy more formal titles like government relations specialists or vice-president in charge of public affairs, etc. They often bring their clients and patrons to town for receptions to "meet your legislator."

Receptions are stand-up affairs where a fellow can nibble on chicken wings, consume pimiento cheese spread over Ritz crackers, stab at little weenies floating in barbecue sauce and enjoy other such edibles while engaging in polite chatter with locals from back home about the weather and the communist menace and finally get around to discussing House Bill such and such to lower the price of eggs in Carthage or some similar gibberish, and the honorable representative will nod wisely and assure Jimmy Dale or whoever that he is "on top of that" and "will do all I can." Which doesn't mean in legislative speak that the honorable will vote for it or help get it out of committee. It just means he will do all he can.

The special interests will give you enough free liquor and wine and beer at these receptions to kill a mule. Other than mastering the plumbing at the Sun-N-Sand Resort Motel, the second most important skills the new representative must develop are certain legislative reception standards. First, you don't have to attend all of 'em. There are two or three every night, scattered here and there about town and it just ain't good for a fellow's health to make 'em all. Second, get a designated driver. Several members should ride together. Harvey Moss from Alcorn County, my true-blue teetotaling friend, was always willing to put up with a car load of us. My long-time roommate, Warner McBride, from Panola County, was also most gracious in looking out for his friends. The new gentleman from Itawamba didn't want to end up as the prize trophy for a rookie Jackson cop.

The reception sponsors usually have a table at the entrance to their soiree with tags bearing the names of the governor and the lieutenant governor and all the members of the House and Senate. If you decide to skip the Mississippi Farm Bureau reception or the Greater Lucedale Sling-Shot Manufacturers Association gala to go to a movie instead, it is a good thing to ask a friend to pick up your name tag so you won't get one of those "We came to Jackson for our 'Squirrel Hunters for Jesus Association' reception and are very sorry we didn't see you" letters. So make sure someone picks up that name tag for you.

Well just imagine the effect these nightly parties may have on a fine upstanding man or woman sent down to Jackson by the good folks up at Mud Creek. The fawning attention, glittering conversation and free food and whiskey can quickly go to a fellow's head. This life has been the downfall of some.

It is quite a sight to watch freshmen legislators adapt to their first few weeks in the Capitol. Our freshman may take the oath wearing cowboy boots and a big-buckled belt with his name on it. This doesn't last long. In two or three weeks, he will be wearing monogrammed starched white shirts under J.C. Penney's best pin-striped suit. Soon enough we all look like undertakers.

And if a fellow keeps making the rounds of all the receptions, in another two or three weeks he will detect a slight tremble in his once steady hands; his lips will be chapped; he has trouble keeping up with his keys; and he has a chronic headache. It's wake-up time! At this point, the new Honorable will either slow down on the extra-curricular activities and get a grip on reality or he will just keep diving deeper and deeper into the pitfalls of legislative ignominy. And someday suffer a lonely crash back to planet earth.

Woe unto the legislator who convinces himself that all this attention is really deserved or that the lobbyists and influence peddlers don't labor behind selfish motives. A fellow must soon learn to put some distance between his social life and his legislative responsibilities. The former legislative leader Butch Lambert had some advice for freshmen legislators which still rings true today. "Son, if you cain't drink their whiskey, eat their steaks, smoke their cigars and vote against 'em the next morning, you won't ever be worth a damn in the Mississippi Legislature."

The freshman legislator must finally admit that his newfound friends may not have his long term best interests at heart. So often in life, and especially in public life, we mistake the office we hold for ourselves. It becomes our sense of being. The new office-holder would be wise to remember that those fawning compliments and little favors received just might not be as plentiful as manna from Heaven if the Honorable so and so didn't have Senator or Representative tagged to his or her name. I know. For I now live in the land of the walking dead. I am . . . (shudder) . . . *a former Representative.*

A former Representative's old friends don't come 'round much anymore. Mississippi State no longer sends free cheese at Christmas. Ole Miss will take you off their free football ticket list. You no longer get free tomato plants from the Co-operative Extension Service. Yes, it is very lonely in the land of the walking dead. The little kindnesses and favors and attentions which once seemed only natural . . . yea for my sacrifices, I was entitled to them . . . are now only memories fading slowly into the past.

Senatorial Privilege

House members learn soon enough that they are somehow inferior to Senators. Somehow the title "Representative Mills" lacks the regnant solemnity or ringing majesty of "SENATOR Foghorn Boregard" or such. Though both Representatives and Senators hail from the same hollers and enclaves, there is certainly a difference in the way the two offices are perceived by the public (and by the Senators).

Individuals elected to the House generally retain their plebian virtues. Not so with Senators. Something strange and wonderful occurs when a shoe clerk or part-time preacher or retired school teacher gets elected to the Mississippi Senate.

The evolution from common man to esteemed and worthy SENATOR begins when our Cincinnatus Mississippiana gets off his tractor and drives down to the Capitol on the first Tuesday after the first Monday every fourth year to take an oath that he will read the Mississippi Constitution (and if he can't read, he swears that he will have someone read it to him. I ain't joking. This is in the oath.) and someone in the Capitol tells him (or her) which side of the building houses the Senate and our hero stumbles into the Senate elevator (which still has a doorman!) and rides that elevator up to the majestic third floor of the Mississippi Capitol and the doorman opens the elevator door and our newly minted servant of the people steps out of the elevator and three or four lobbyists leap toward him (or her, there is no such thing as a Senatress) with smiles beaming wider than the Old Tombigbee River in flood season and with hands outstretched in good Christian fellowship, say those wonderfully magic words: "Hello, Senator." Most startled citizens, not yet even sworn in, might normally step back from such an assault. My goodness! Isn't this a little much? But . . . Wait! . . . What did they say? . . . Senator! . . . Hmmmm . . . It certainly has a nice ring to the ear . . . Such well-balanced vowels . . . Sen . . . A . . . Tor . . . And it goes with my name so well . . . How fitting!

You are now witnessing, my friend, the birth of a Senator . . . Watch as our hero straightens his back a

The Sun-N-Sand Years

bit and stands a little taller. . . . He now spreads his shoulders a little wider . . . Why, he may find preening and posturing somewhat fitting and acceptable in this newfound delight! . . . What a sense of well-being one feels by the very mention of that title . . . Senator!! It is better than a narcotic! The effect is like one of those new good feeling prescription drugs that always end in *-cet* . . . Why it can make one feel rather . . . Romanish!

A new life has begun! Bring on the togas!

A case in point. Representative "Bo" Robinson and Representative "Billy" Bowles and I were invited to face a crowd of angry Monroe County school teachers back home in Nettleton one fine Saturday morning in February. The three of us showed up on time to get a full dose of the democratic process. Senator Bryan ("Hob," not William Jennings) arrived halfway through the agony and announced that he was tickled to be there and thanked the teachers for inviting him and stated that he had to "get up the road to meet with some other teachers in West Point." Was he penalized for arriving late or cutting out early? No way! The teachers all just glowed with good will as they thanked Senator Bryan to high heavens for taking the time to show up and spend a little time with the common folks. They wished him well as he departed. They then rewarded Bo and Billy and me for being on time and staying for the full meeting by telling us exactly what the teacher's union would do for *us* if we didn't "toe the line."

But our Senator soon finds that government pay for

senatorial privileges is not quite commensurate with the honor bestowed. In fact, horror of horrors, Senators are paid exactly the same as those lower forms of legislative life, Representatives. But Senate districts are so much larger! And Senators must answer to three times as many people! And therein lies the rub, as Hamlet would say. It costs more to be a Senator! *Ipso fatso*, some Senators quickly warm up to the lobbyists. And since there are far fewer Senators to stroke than Representatives, the lobbyists find it much more cost effective to "sponsor" a member of the upper house and let the commoners in the lower house shift for themselves.

At noon in the Capitol, on a typical day, certain ritu-

Senator Hob Bryan and Mills

als are played out as sure as clockwork. Three or four House members will cross the parking lot, unescorted, hunkered down against the elements in inclement weather, headed for a cheap blue plate special somewhere within walking distance. In the old days it would have been at the Sun-N-Sand. Not so for Senators. Many rarely eat without a "sponsor" and then only at the finest downtown restaurants.

I was standing in the Capitol foyer with my fellow Itawamba County Representative Jerry Wilburn one day around noon when we spied a lobbyist step off the Senate elevator with seven or eight Senators in tow. "Well looka there!," Jerry said. "Those Senators look just like them little ducks struttin' through the lobby of the Peabody Hotel!"

There are also important differences between the two chambers in how a bill becomes law. In the House, sooner or later, every bill gets "thrayshed out" on the floor. House members who wish to be effective must develop fairly articulate oratorical skills to survive and excel in the frequent free-for-alls which pass for legislative debates. Every bill eventually gets publicly discussed and voted on, by yes or no vote, red light or green, as the members "go on the board," thereby making their record.

Senators do *not* go on the board. They enjoy a parliamentary procedure known as "the morning roll call." This means that Senators don't have to vote on every bill that comes before them. If a particularly troublesome piece of legislation comes up, someone will simply move that "this bill be passed on the morning roll call." It is thus presumed that everyone who was present in the morning when the session began approved the bill. No formal vote is taken. If a Senator later wishes to hide his support or opposition to a particular bill, why, he can say, "that passed on morning roll call. I would have voted against it if I had a chance." This is how many troublesome matters are handled in the Senate. But bring up a bill raising hunting and fishing licenses or extending duck season and they will raise the roof demanding a roll call vote!

Jerry Wilburn once opined that since the Senate preferred passing most of its legislation by morning roll call, "We ought to just let 'em wear powdered wigs and debate all day . . . but take away their right to vote. They're scared to use it anyway."

In Search of a Legacy

I chaired the Judiciary "A" Committee in the Mississippi House in the early 1990's. A Chairman has an opportunity to meet some mighty fine folks from throughout Mississippi and around the nation. Lawyers, doctors and business-folk often have matters to be considered by the Judiciary Committee. The attentive Chairman of any committee can find many occasions to be helpful to individuals and special interests alike. The best deals occur when both the

Chairman and the lobbyist come away with a warm, fuzzy feeling of mutual gain.

Judicial Reform was a major issue when I chaired Judiciary "A." Our committee considered a bill to create a new Court of Appeals whose judges would be appointed, rather than elected. This legislation reflected my own judicial philosophy (or bias, depending upon one's point of view). I have long believed that judges, particularly appellate court judges, should be appointed rather than elected. This does not mean, of course that I believe all public servants should be appointed. For instance, it goes without saying that Senators and Representatives should be elected since our representative form of government demands that law*makers* represent the will of the people, at least theoretically. Judges however represent the rule of law; not popular will. Judges must act independent of the whims and fads of popular opinion or the inevitable influence of special interests in elections. The only way I know to prevent this unwanted outside influence on the judiciary is to create appointed judgeships.

Our legislation providing for an appointed Court of Appeals was called up for floor action. I spent some time at the podium explaining the need for an additional appellate court and how the new court would function. I appealed to the members' sense of justice by explaining that the Supreme Court had a three years' backlog at the time. I mentioned the old saw that "justice delayed is justice denied" and may have mumbled some other homilies for the boys and was feeling pretty good about the bill's chance for success when the time came for debate.

My cause was just. My presentation had been eloquent. My team was in place. The Committee, under my chairmanship, had yet to lose a floor vote. Things looked mighty good. It was then that I noticed my friend, the Honorable Tommy Horne of Meridian, one of my sub-committee chairmen, standing in back of the Chamber, seeking recognition. This gave me some concern. Tommy suffered from a sometimes intolerable streak of independence. Nevertheless, I waylaid my fears by presuming that Tommy sought recognition for the purpose of asking me some friendly questions. In baseball parlance, I hoped he was going to throw me some softballs.

Some days the legislature more resembles professional wrestling than a deliberative body. If TV cameras are present or the galleries are too full, some members just have to "show out." If there is a chance of getting in the papers or on TV, certain members can't resist the temptation to get up and squawk about the "little man" while others may feel the Lord move them to speak out for school teachers or against county unit or what have you. Tommy Horne wasn't that way at all. He didn't speak just for the cameras. He was a true believer . . . in whatever he believed.

Tommy Horne is an American original from Lauderdale County. He had served off and on as a legislator for over 20 years by the time our paths first crossed. He had also once served as an elected Justice of the Peace, so in all fairness, he had had some experience with electing judges. Philosophically, Tommy despised banks, railroads, insurance companies and anything that smacked of elitism or privilege. He was one of the most effective voices for the mythical "little man" to ever serve in the Mississippi Legislature. Tommy wanted to elect everybody, probably even public school teachers and game wardens. Let the people decide!

In the 1990's Tommy was the powerful, and feared, Chairman of the House Rules Committee. If you crossed Tommy Horne, your bill to name the local Co-Operative Extension Center after somebody's deceased uncle might die on the calendar. Men like Tommy keep the system honest. But they create a good deal of mischief in the process.

"Will the gentleman yield?" Tommy's voice boomed through the chamber.

"Certainly, I yield to my friend, the gentleman from Lauderdale County."

"Mr. Chairman, would you explain to the members how judges were to be selected in this bill we have before us, as it was drafted and introduced?"

"As you know, Gentleman from Lauderdale, it provided for elected judges."

"And would you tell us, Mr. Chairman, how it got changed to appointed judges?"

"I believe the sub-committee amended it to provide for the governor to appoint the judges," I replied.

"And just who, Mr. Chairman decides which bills go to that sub-committee?"

"Why, of course, I do," I said.

"And tell me, Mr. Chairman, who appointed the members of the sub-committee?"

"Why of course, I did, Gentleman from Lauderdale."

"That's all I need to know," he said.

Tommy then walked purposefully to the podium, nodded respectfully to me, took a deep breath for emphasis, and gave a stem-winding, bridge-burning, hand-wringing speech against the evils of appointing judges. He cited *Marbury v. Madison, Brown v. Board of Education* and *Miranda* as clear examples of the evils committed by appointed judges. He appealed to reason. He appealed to emotion. He appealed to self-interest. He reminded the members of past favors granted and future favors that might be denied.

Tommy finally appealed to institutional jealousy (always popular with the members) by complaining of all those cards we had to hand out to get elected and all those speakin's and rallies we had to attend, begging for votes. He closed his oration with a call to "make those judges get out there on the hustings and eat that half-raw chicken and those cold taters and buy those old ladies' club cookbooks they don't need just like we have to do." (The obvious moral being if democracy is barely tolerable for us, let's make the judges suffer too.)

The members loved it, of course. My bill got only 18 or 19 votes. Tommy carried the day and judges on the Intermediate Court of Appeals are now elected.

How 'bout Some Milk with These Cookies?

It's a big deal for a legislator to receive any trifling attention from the Governor. If more governors understood this fact of Capitol life, more executive programs would be adopted in Mississippi. The little folks in the House and Senate are more than happy to go along with many gubernatorial proposals as long as the governor will give the individual members a bit of personal face time in advance and is willing to share a little of the credit for mutual accomplishments. Unfortunately such cooperation has been noticeably missing in state government in recent administrations.

Governor Kirk Fordice was not a very compromising character. He did, however, share some moments of camaraderie with lesser beings. He invited me to join him and Lieutenant Governor Eddie Briggs and House Speaker Tim Ford on an industry recruiting trip to New York City in the late spring of 1993. We were committed to two days of meeting with Japanese and Canadian industrialists at various fancy restaurants around town with our nights to be spent in the Waldorf Astoria Hotel. I had never been to New York, so this was a red-letter event for me.

We flew to New York in a narrow aluminum tube, also known as the State Lear jet. The cramped passenger seats in back of the plane forced us to sit knee to knee. The Governor and I sat bumping up against Speaker Ford and Lieutenant Governor Briggs.

I was just getting to know the Governor at the time

and found him easy to like. I had previously served for nearly ten years in state government with Ford and Briggs. By nature, both of them are also fairly easy to get along with. All three, like me, can be rather loquacious on social occasions. Naturally I assumed our flight would consist of a couple of hours of delightful and witty conversation about the vagaries and vicissitudes of our shared responsibilities. Such was not the case.

Many descriptions have been applied to Kirk Fordice. Some have called him blunt or stubborn. Others have said he was arrogant. My legislative buddy, Barney Schoby, once said Governor Fordice was ". . . like a cat with a barbed-wire tail." I don't disagree with these assessments, though I personally found him to be quite charming. He exuded a can-do spirit and bubbled enthusiasm. He genuinely liked the people of Mississippi and I believe the voters sensed this, enabling him to share a mutual affection with a majority of the voters each time he ran for office. Being an engineer, he was always open to better ways of doing things. However, he was not anxious to master the nuances and niceties of certain legislative traditions, such as the old practice of "I'll scratch your back if you'll scratch mine." He simply assumed that all issues should stand on their own merits. The shortest way to the truth of an issue, in Fordice's mind, was direct. And this direct style sometimes became confrontational.

I have a notion that the best public servants are those folks who have been successful in something in life *before* seeking public office. Such men and women are not as easily seduced by the pomp and prestige attendant to holding public office. Nor are they as likely to be swayed by the shifting moods of public opinion. Their sense of self is not wrapped up in hanging on to public office. Consequently, such office-holders are more likely to speak and vote their convictions, rather than what they perceive to be popular at any given moment. Kirk Fordice had been successful in life before he sought public office. He had excelled in the military, in engineering and in private business, long before he became governor. In all these endeavors, he was always the boss. He was accustomed to giving orders and assumed they would be followed. He brought this assumption to public office.

Captain Kirk, as we sometimes called him, saw himself as *The* Chief Executive Officer of the State of Mississippi. In many instances, he viewed legislators and senators as junior executives, elected by the people to help him enact and carry out his policies. Of course, Eddie Briggs and Tim Ford, like most members of the legislature, had their own ideas about the role of the Governor in public life. The House and Senate leaders had attained their positions without Kirk's help. Consequently, they were not anxious to defer in public or private to the Governor's directives on state policy. The Ford and Briggs views were consistent with the opinions of most other Mississippi legislators who considered their offices as important checks and balances on the whims of any chief executive. At the time I understood and shared these views theoretically but had not grasped how such theories might spill over into private relationships between the separate branches of government. Until I got on the State jet.

We were barely airborne, having hardly said "howdy do," when the co-pilot tip-toed down the tube and installed a small round table between our knees. He then set sandwiches and cold drinks before us. Since the sandwiches were all the same, we had no dispute as to who got what. After the main course, the co-pilot next set a plastic plate with four cookies before us. They looked mighty good and I wanted one badly, but being sensitive to my rank among the other three, I waited for them to get a cookie before I reached for mine. No one moved. I thought perhaps Tim and Eddie, like me, were waiting for the Governor to take the first cookie. After all, he was the Chief Executive of the State of Mississippi! But he didn't reach for a cookie.

We sat in silence, precious minutes slipping away as the jet hurtled toward New York. I feared the co-pilot would soon take our plate away and order us to prepare to land before we ate our cookies. Yet no action was being taken and no cookies were being eaten. (Do you see the irony here?)

Finally the Governor spoke in a good-natured but authoritative tone, clearly expecting the Lieutenant Governor to immediately comply with his directive: "Eddie, taste one of those cookies and tell me if they have peanuts. I don't like peanuts in cookies."

Eddie chose not to do so, saying, "I don't like peanuts either, Governor."

Unfazed, Kirk said, "Tim, taste those cookies and tell me if they have peanuts in them."

The Speaker replied pleasantly, "I don't care for a cookie right now, Governor."

As my grandma would have said, "They Lawd!" A Constitutional impasse was occurring. The Governor, having been firmly rebuffed, said nothing further. We eyed the cookies. Finally I could take it no longer. I reached for a cookie, tasted a delightful homemade teacake, and then lied to my companions. "Sorry, men. Full of peanuts."

I ate all the cookies before we landed. Several morals may be gleaned from this anecdote but I will leave it to you to sort them out.

How It All Began

Jerry Wilburn and I were sitting around the Sun-N-Sand pool one evening when he asked, "Little Mills, have you ever wondered why the people of Itawamba County sent me and you to the Legislature at the same time?"

"Why, yes," I responded. "It is really amazing that the good folks of Itawamba County would send you and me to the Mississippi Legislature at the same time. We come from different worlds. The Good Lord split our county in half with the Tombigbee River. The Federal government wasn't satisfied with the Good Lord's work, so they matched the Good Lord and split it again with the Tennessee-Tombigbee Waterway. I am from Fulton, a relatively progressive little hamlet on the east side of the rivers. You were hand-spanked and corn-bread fed west of the rivers in Mantachie. And never shall these two meet. I went to Ole Miss, got myself a law degree and enjoy some prominence in Northeast Mississippi as a rising young lawyer. You on the other hand are a Mississippi State man. And, to tell the truth, Jerry, you are just one step ahead of driving a pulp-wood truck. But there is no need to go any further," I said. "I really can't see how the good folks of Itawamba County sent you and me to the Mississippi Legislature at the same time."

"Well, I'll tell you," he said.

"Back around the turn of the century, a jake-legged preacher ran for the Mississippi Legislature in one of them floater districts on the Tombigbee River. His campaign platform was *'my lips have never tasted bonded whiskey . . . nor a strange woman's breath.'* The folks thought that was a fine campaign platform, so they sent the preacher to Jackson.

"The preacher moved into a room on the third floor of the old King Edward Hotel, and, being in the Legislature, started drankin' after about six weeks. He was embarrassed about that for a while (violated his campaign platform and all) but soon enough got used to it.

"As the preacher settled into the Jackson lifestyle, he

became more self-conscious of his 'sartorial splendor,' or lack thereof. So he went to Montgomery-Ward's to buy himself a 'matching suit.' It was there that he met a girdle saleswoman who helped him pick out a fine three piece suit, complete with a gold watch-chain for his vest pocket. (Since he didn't have a gold watch, he just punched a hole through a Liberty half-dollar and ran his chain through it.) He told the helpful girdle saleswoman that he was a member of the Mississippi Legislature and invited her to a reception that night. (He didn't mention that he was a preacher too. And married.) At first the preacher told everyone she was his 'niece from back home.' But it wasn't long before the girdle saleswoman moved in with the preacher, who now preferred to be called 'the Gentleman from Tombigbee.' He just had the one room on the third floor and they had to share a bathroom down the hall, but it was a sight better than the folks back home had.

"Back in those days the Legislative sessions were unlimited and it was hard to get home on weekends. Instead the preacher would write a letter every week or so for the local paper to tell the folks what all he was doing for their benefit down in Jackson. Said he knew he was new to Jackson, and all, but if they would let him stay a few more terms and get him some seniority that, Lord willing, he would get all the public school teachers a pay raise and lower taxes for all the farmers and might even be able to get a shirt factory to locate somewhere. And everybody thought he was doing a mighty good job.

(The Gentleman from Tombigbee failed to sense approaching doom.)

"Around mid-summer the Legislature finally adjourned so the farmers could go home and make their crops. The Gentleman from Tombigbee didn't want to go home, as he was a preacher and didn't have a crop to make, so he just stayed on at the King Edward Hotel with the girdle saleswoman. He kept writin' letters home to the papers tellin' how, on behalf of the good folks of his District, he was stayin' on to be on some special study committees.

"Since all the parties had ended, the girdle-saleswoman became bored with the Gentleman from Tombigbee. So she ran off with a Singer Sewing Machine salesman. Left a note for the Gentleman from Tombigbee sayin' how special he was and how she would never forget him, and all, but she just wanted to 'see the country'.

"The Gentleman from Tombigbee was shocked when he found the note. Grief swallowed his spirit. He sat despondent and alone in his room in the old King Edward Hotel, crying for days and doing little more than drinking bonded whiskey. His depression would not go away. He truly mourned. In another week or two, he had other concerns.

"It turns out that the girdle saleswoman had left the Gentleman with a painful infection. What we would today call a *socially transmitted disease*. An STD! The Gentleman no longer grieved. He was now truly horrified. He knew he couldn't go home. The people would know that he had violated his campaign promises. And he was ashamed to go to a doctor. Him bein' a preacher and all. So he just stayed on by himself at the old King Edward Hotel, drankin' and sufferin' and writin' letters home to the good folks of his District about what a fine job he was doing for 'em in Jackson. They were so proud of him.

"Late summer led to fall, and the leaves fell and all the South prepared for the coming winter sleep. But not the Gentleman from Tombigbee. He could find no peace. His condition worsened. As did the drinking. He could not return home. So, as the days became shorter and the breeze became crisper and brown leaves blew in through the open window of the lonely room on the third floor of the old King Edward Hotel and sounds of Christmas cheer began to jingle on the sidewalks of Jackson, the Gentleman began to sort of just fade away. Finally, a week before Christmas, he died from a broken heart. And a severe case of clap.

"The folks in the hotel found him after a day or two and dressed his carcass in his good suit that the girdle saleswoman had picked out for him. They stole his gold watch-chain and the Liberty half-dollar and tied a name-tag to the Gentleman's toe and put him in a pine box and shipped him home by train. He reached home the day before Christmas.

"Great sorrow filled the region as the pine box was unloaded from the freight car. The Gentleman's pallbearers placed the box on the back of an old wagon, which, pulled by four matched mules, led a procession of thousands of grieving Tombigbee Country folk up an old graveled road, headed far, far into the country, seeking a little white church in a valley, near a cedar thicket, where his fathers lay. There to properly bury the Gentleman from Tombigbee.

"The day of mourning was freezing cold. Hundreds stood outside the little church. Though they could not hear the service, they didn't want to miss the event. Not a soul left before the burial.

"They brought the body to the grave. The red ground was hard as concrete. The crowd watched silently as the pallbearers began chipping away at the frozen earth. The work was slow. It was as though the earth was not yet ready to receive his remains. The pallbearers began to tire. Silent voters stepped forward, one by one, to take their turns with the pick and shovel, all done to dig a proper grave for the Gentleman from Tombigbee.

"Finally they lowered his casket into the ground. Not a whimper was heard as the men took their turns shoveling the red dirt, a spadeful at a time, into the pit. It seemed bottomless. Finally, as the last shovel full of dirt fell and they finished their labors, gently mounding the red dirt above the grave, grown men broke down and cried, saying they 'would never send another *good* man to the Mississippi Legislature.'

"And that is why, Little Mills, the good folks living along the Tombigbee River sent me and you to Jackson."

The Life and Times of A.C. "Butch" Lambert, Sr.

Some lives are patterns for us to follow. These pattern-setters have special gifts of the spirit which brighten our lives. Butch Lambert was one of these gifted folks. He was a large-framed man with the carriage and movements of a life-long athlete. By the 1980's, when I knew Butch, his coarse walnut brown hair had grayed like a dark wintry afternoon, adding depth to his constant, timid smile which broke straight across his wide square face. His eyes, brown as chocolate, betrayed a tender sadness.

Some public figures are consumed by titles: Coach, Judge, Governor, Senator, etc. Title being important to them, such folks often become enslaved to the institution from which they gain prestige. They can't live without it. But our really great public figures are unaffected by title, rank or privilege. These rare souls are large enough in spirit to affect the institutions. Butch Lambert was one of these. He had the courage to simply be himself, whether in business, athletics or government. Butch was the same, whether dancing with kings or dining with potato eaters. Let me give you a personal example.

I was sworn into the Mississippi House of Representatives on the first Tuesday following the first Monday in January of 1984. I ran for office on a "Reform" theme and had committed myself to vote to "change the Rules." The so-called reformers were attempting to change the House Rules which allowed the Speaker to hold office indefinitely and to appoint all committees, among other things. The first person to vote to change the rules on the roll-call vote was my former law school colleague, John Grisham. (We called him Gris'm.) My vote was the second cast. The 26 of us who voted to change the rules were later tagged the "Gang of 26." Speaker Buddie Newman rewarded the gang members, many of whom were young lawyers like myself, with generally poor committee assignments. Most of us were appointed to the less-than-prestigious Agriculture Committee or Military Affairs where we spent four years worrying over various seed and feed issues and what we would do if the Yankees invaded again. In fact, there were more lawyers serving on the Agriculture Committee that term than on the either of the Judiciary Committees.

John and I had a lot of time to kill. He used his profitably, toiling away in his second floor Sun-N-Sand room, working on his classic novel, *A Time To Kill*. John is now one of Mississippi's finest ambassadors of good will.

But I am getting ahead of myself. Prior to taking the

oath of office, I was anxious about what role, if any, I would play in the new legislature. I was also physically ill. I was running a high fever a few days before the legislature was to go into session and was so sick that Mona had to pack my suitcase for me. I slept in my pajamas and house coat in the back seat of our car as she drove us to Jackson on the Monday before the first Tuesday.

I was still running a high fever when Mona woke me on Tuesday morning about an hour before we were to take our oaths. I showered and shaved and managed to get my good suit on when I realized that I had no shoes. I had worn my sunlight yellow house shoes to Jackson. We had neglected to bring any other shoes! Since I was to be sworn into office in less than thirty minutes, I hurried to the front desk to ask the manager where I could most likely purchase a pair of black dress shoes in the next fifteen minutes. There I saw State Tax Commissioner Butch Lambert coming out of the restaurant.

I didn't know Butch too well at the time, though I had recently met with him about my impending vote to change the Rules. Though Butch was close to the Speaker, Buddie Newman, he did not try to influence me in any way other than to tell me that he thought I would be "better off" if I didn't vote to change the Rules. Subsequent events proved him right. (I was never close to Speaker Newman who hailed from Issaquena County, but did learn a phrase from him, *"What you say, Scannell-bugger!"* I have no idea what this means.

I believe it evidences surprise or delight.)

Butch stopped at the counter as I was speaking to the manager and asked how I was doing and was I excited about getting sworn in. I said, "Butch, I'm not doing very well. I'm running a high fever and don't feel too good."

He looked me over carefully, then said, "Mike, I hate to tell you this, but not only are you running a fever, but it looks like you have on your house shoes too."

I laughed and said, "Yeah. I'm trying to find a store nearby right now to buy a new pair of shoes."

"You don't have time," he said. "There aren't any shoe stores around here. Take mine." And he pulled off his big black leather dress shoes which were about two sizes too large, and handed them to me. I chuckled and put them on, and handed him my bright yellow house shoes, which he put on his feet and strolled on out of the motel, headed to his office in the Woolfolk building. I doubt Buddie Newman found any humor in the fact that I "filled Butch's shoes" on my first day in the Mississippi House of Representatives.

• • •

Aaron Colus "Butch" Lambert was born in 1923 near the rural Tishomingo County village of Holcut. His birthplace now lies at the bottom of the Tennessee-Tombigbee Waterway. As Chairman of the Ways and Means Committee in the Mississippi House of Representatives, Butch Lambert wrote the legislation that built the bridges now spanning that river. These bridges are a fitting tribute to the man. He spent his life building bridges between people.

Butch grew up a country boy, and country boys in the Depression years knew hardship and privation first hand. Many Mississippi farm families in those days were literally rootless. Butch never let the humble circumstances of his birth prevent him from making a positive impact on the world around him. Many reared in privation and need become bitter and mean-spirited. Not Butch. He is proof that the poorest soil sometimes produces the sweetest fruit. That all souls may choose to rise above their times.

One way Butch enriched the lives of those around him was through his stories. One of his favorites bears repeating.

Butch's Aunt Maudie had a little country store in Holcut where Butch hung out as a child, listening to the gossip and tales related by loafers sitting around Aunt Maudie's wood-burning, pot-belly stove. Late one afternoon a fellow driving a big shiny Buick pulled up to the gas pumps and started pumping gas. He drew the loafers' attention for a number of reasons. First, he was driving the finest car any of them had ever seen. Second, his right arm was in a sling. Finally, it appeared to the brethren gathered around the stove that the fellow had his shirt on backwards. They were certainly puzzled as to who this character might be. After some discussion, one of the loafers named Jim volunteered to go out and ascertain just who this character might be.

"Howdy, neighbor," Jim said with a smile.

"Why hello, my friend."

"Where's that car from?"

"Memphis, Tennessee."

"I say. What you do for a living?"

"I'm a priest."

"I swannee," said Jim. "What's a priest?"

"The leader of the local church in the Catholic faith. Something like a preacher in the Protestant faith."

"Oh, I see," said Jim. "Well why you got your shirt on backwards?"

The priest chuckled. "This isn't a shirt. This is what we call a habit. You might call it my uniform. Much as a preacher would wear a necktie."

"Well," said Jim. "What you doing down here?"

"My church rented a cabin near here for a few days. We are on a retreat."

"What's a retreat?"

"It is a time when we go off to an isolated place for intense community worship. Something like a revival, I guess."

"I see," said Jim. "Can I ask you one more question?"

"Sure," the priest said.

"How'd you break your arm?"

The priest chuckled as he replaced the gas nozzle. "That is a little embarrassing. I was standing on a commode changing a light bulb when I fell and broke it."

"I see," said Jim.

The priest paid for his gas and pulled away. As he was leaving, one of the loafer's neighbors asked, "Well,

Jim, who was that?"

"Catholic priest," Jim said.

"What's a priest?"

"Kinda like a preacher I reckon," Jim said.

"Why'd he have his shirt on backwards?"

"That ain't a shirt, that's a habit. Same as one of our preachers wearing a necktie."

"Well what's he doin' here?"

"Says he's on a retreat," Jim replied.

"What's a retreat?"

"Kinda like where they all go off and have a revival."

The boys around the stove sat digesting this information. Finally one of them asked, "Well, how did he break his arm?"

"Said he fell off a commode," Jim said.

"What's a commode?"

"Hell if I know," Jim said. *"I ain't Catholic."*

• • •

The Lamberts left Holcut for the more urbane environs of Fulton, where Butch became an outstanding high school athlete at Itawamba Agricultural High School, where he was graduated in 1941. The next year he married his high school sweetheart, the fifteen-year old Ida Gilliland (they would have four children, Butch, Jr., Vicki, Amy and Scotty) and joined the United States Navy. While in the Navy, Butch played center on the Great Lakes National Service football team, then coached by the famous NFL Coach, Paul Brown. One of his teammates and close friends on this team was future Notre Dame Coach, Ara Parseghian. After the war, Butch entered Ole Miss, where he played for the Rebels under Coach Johnny Vaught.

Upon graduation from college, Butch took a job as assistant football coach and head basketball coach at Southwest Junior College in Summit, Mississippi. He was then called home to Fulton, where he became the first head football coach and athletic director at Itawamba Junior College. Butch left coaching in 1952 to work for the Mississippi Tax Commission. Around this same time he also became certified as a referee for athletic events in the Southeastern Conference.

Butch officiated college football and basketball games from 1953 through 1982. He called four NCAA regional basketball tournaments and 12 post-season football bowl games, including the Sugar, Bluebonnet, Liberty, Gator, Orange and Independence Bowls. Two of the bowl games he officiated were for a national championship. Butch's partner in most of these games was a Tennessee lawyer, Harrold Johnson, whom Butch called "Harl." "Butch and Harl" stories still circulate among those familiar with college football officiating lore.

Butch and Harold were traveling to Tuscaloosa to call an Alabama game in the late 1960's when Harold mentioned that the legendary Bama head coach, Bear Bryant was having an awful lot of success with little players like Kenny Stabler. Butch said he didn't think that approach would work in basketball. "For instance," he asked Harold, "If the Bear was coaching

Butch Lambert

basketball, do you think he could guard Wilt Chamberlain with a five-nine center?"

Before the game, Harold and Butch went through both teams' dressing rooms. When they got to the Bama dressing room, they noticed the boys seemed uptight. Butch thought he would loosen them up by asking the players, "Do any of you boys think you can guard Wilt Chamberlain?" The boys just sat on their benches, staring blank-faced at Butch. No one responded but the Bear, who said, "Butch, this is a football game. Don't be bringing that basketball foolishness in here just before we play. Now you get on out there and let me talk to these boys myself!" Butch left the dressing room with his feelings a little hurt.

The band played the National Anthem and Butch stood at handsome attention in his striped shirt and white pants, holding his cap over his heart. As always, tears stained his cheeks as he remembered those who sacrificed so much for freedom. (Butch had soul).

The game was tight at the half. As the players and officials were trotting off the field for the half-time break, Butch felt someone tug his sleeve. He stopped and turned. It was Bear Bryant. "Now Butch," he said. "I don't want you to get the wrong idea about what I said in there before the game."

Butch thought to himself, "Doggone if the Bear ain't about to apologize."

Then the Bear said, "Like I said Butch, don't take me wrong. Wilt Chamberlain *can* be guarded."

• • •

Butch and Harold were calling a Kentucky Wildcats basketball game when Harold called a foul on one of the Kentucky players. It was Harold's first college basketball game. As the teams trotted down court, Adolph Rupp, the colorful Wildcats head coach, asked Butch, "Who's that other sonofabitch you got helping you?"

Butch just shrugged and ignored Rupp's slander of Harold as he trotted on down court. He then stopped cold in the middle of the gymnasium. It had dawned on him that he had been slandered too. He spun on his heels, pointed his finger at Rupp and shouted, "Adolph, don't you never call me a sonofabitch again!"

• • •

Butch's most famous officiating moment came in the 1978 Gator Bowl where the Clemson Tigers, led by a young upstart head coach named Danny Ford, were playing the Ohio State Buckeyes, led by the legendary Woody Hayes. Late in the fourth quarter a Clemson player intercepted a Buckeye pass, sealing a 17-15 win for the Tigers. The play ended near the Ohio State bench. Hayes, who was standing nearby, grabbed the Clemson player and threw a haymaker at him. In the melee that followed, Butch threw his flag; his cap; and Woody out of the game . . . all on national TV. This play ended Hayes' coaching career.

Despite the headiness obtained from consorting with football legends and being on national TV nearly every weekend, Butch never forgot his momma whom he tried to telephone or visit after every game. She was proud of Butch (she always called him Aaron) and didn't miss a game on TV if he was officiating. She had been watching the Gator Bowl when Butch threw Woody out of the game. When Butch came by for his weekly visit, she asked, "Aaron, I saw you throw that mean ole' coach out of the game after he hit that boy. But y'all were having words too. What was he saying to you?"

Butch replied, "Momma, I cain't tell you exactly what he was saying. But it wasn't very nice about you."

• • •

Butch was line judge in a game between Mississippi State and the Texas Tech Red Raiders. Tech's brilliant running back, Donnie Anderson, dominated the game. (He would later star for the Green Bay Packers). Every time Tech scored, a cannon in the end zone BOOMED! and the "Red Raider," a masked rider dressed like Zorro, complete with sword and cape, came flying out of the stadium exit on his horse, his cape waving behind as he raced twice around the field. This theatrical display occurred several times during the game, later inspiring Butch to wax poetic.

Late in the fourth quarter, Tech had the ball on the State six-yard line and was threatening to score again. The ball was snapped. The quarterback handed off to Anderson, who crashed into the line and fell across the five-yard line. Butch jumped from his crouch and raised his hands, signaling a touchdown.

The crowd went wild, the cannon went off and the Red Raider took off around the field. Harold trotted over to Butch and asked, "What in the WORLD were you thinking?"

Butch said, "I got confused! I thought the five was the goal line. Now what we gonna do?"

"I ain't gonna do nothin' but watch that horse run around the field first," Harold said. "Then I'm going to the State bench and explain to them what happened, and you are going to the Tech bench and explain it to them."

"I figured you'd make me go over there," Butch said.

Play was halted as Butch trotted across the field to the Tech bench and announced to the head coach:

Reload your cannon,
Remount your horse.
Your boy didn't score,
The ball's on the four!

• • •

In another game, the Memphis State Tigers traveled to Baton Rouge to play Louisiana State University. The LSU Tigers have a well-deserved reputation for being hard to beat in Tiger Stadium. In this particular game, LSU was whipping Memphis State pretty good. Throughout the game, Billy "Spook" Murphy, the Memphis State head coach, had been rather animated and vocal in his opinions about how the game was being called. The referees ignored his taunts for most of the game. Late in the fourth quarter, Butch called a 15 yard penalty on a Memphis State player for unnecessary roughness. As Butch walked off the 15 yards, Murphy ran onto the field, saying ugly things about Butch's momma. Butch threw a flag on him, added another 15 yards to the penalty and ordered the coach back to the bench. Butch began walking off the second 15 yards.

Returning to his bench, Murphy yelled, "I knew we were gonna get - - - -ed when we came down here!"

To which Butch retorted, "Well I don't want you to go home disappointed!" He threw his flag again, called another technical penalty on the Memphis State coach, and marched the ball back yet another 15 yards.

• • •

Former Ole Miss quarterback Archie Manning told me that he always thought Butch liked him but that he didn't realize Butch's partiality until his senior year when Butch refereed the annual Ole Miss spring game, known as "The Red-Blue Game." In those days the Red-Blue game was the 12th game of the

Butch Lambert at work.

season for Ole Miss. It drew nearly as many fans as a regular season game. The two teams were separately coached and practiced separately in closed practices for weeks before the game. A lot of pride was at stake.

Archie was captain of the Red team. His friend Freddie Brister captained the Blue team. Butch came out to meet the captains at mid-field for the coin toss to determine who got the ball first. He reached in his pocket and pulled his hand out empty. "Oh, hell boys," he said. "I forgot to bring a coin. Let's just pick a number between one and ten to decide who gets to choose whether to kick or receive. Freddie, you pick a number between one and ten."

"Five," Freddie said.

"Sorry, Freddie, wrong number," Butch said. "Now, Archie. What do you want to do? Kick or receive?"

• • •

Butch's long service to athletics has been recognized by his peers. The All-American Foundation honors an outstanding college or professional football official each year with presentation of the Butch Lambert Football Official's Award.

• • •

Butch always felt a deep sense of responsibility for the welfare of working folks in North Mississippi. He had been born into hard times and knew the pain of living in need. In addition to his other avocations, Butch served as director of employee relations for

Rockwell International, a Tupelo manufacturing company. He was a natural for this position. As a child in Itawamba County, I often heard Butch named as being responsible for a neighbor or friend "getting on" at Rockwell. He likewise used his position in the Legislature to make sure we got "our fair share" of jobs with the Tax Commission, the Highway Patrol and other state agencies. These jobs were hard to come by in the 1960's, and Butch's greatest legacy may be the number of families who were able to stay in North Mississippi because he helped a bread-winner get a job. If Butch couldn't find a fellow a job, then perhaps the person was unemployable.

• • •

Butch had become so busy with politics and business and sports by the 1970's that he needed to fly to keep his numerous appointments. So he bought a small, single engine Cessna. His little plane added a certain panache, or as we say back home, flash, to Butch's personality. He set a new standard for legislative flamboyance when he became the "Flying Chairman." But his flying skills had certain limitations. He never bothered to get a pilot's license as he didn't want to take a physical. Nevertheless, he was a good daylight pilot who flew like a pigeon. By landmarks.

One of the most popular men to ever serve in the Mississippi House was Ed "Stump" Perry of Oxford. Ed is built like a little tea-pot, short and stout. But he is long on kindness and consideration for others. As a conversationalist, he is worth getting to know. He can discuss Ole Miss football, the philosophy of Nietzsche or the latest hair styles with equal depth and enthusiasm.

A conversation with Ed Perry is like being nibbled by a duck. He likes to touch people as he talks. He just keeps pulling on your elbow or hand 'till you agree with him. He has another delightful habit, when he grasps a point, of looking up at his listener, nodding his head up and down and, with eyes shut, mumbles "iunderstandiunderstandiunderstandBubba. . . ." Everyone is Bubba to Ed. He wears man-sized breeches, cut off at the knees, and has the torso of a wrestler. At the House podium, he is an impressive little giant. Ed was Chairman of the House Appropriations Committee when Butch chaired Ways and Means. They were also Jackson roommates. Ed tells me that Butch worked well with people because, "He was born with a Ph.D. in human nature. He just naturally understood people."

One Sunday morning Speaker Newman called a meeting of his committee chairmen for later that afternoon in Jackson. It must have been something very important because legislative meetings rarely occurred on Sunday. Not even unofficial meetings.

Ed Perry usually caught a ride to Jackson. He had given his much-coveted Capitol parking space to one of the employees and depended upon other members of the House to give him a ride to work.

Ed didn't want to miss the Speaker's meeting but he

didn't have a ride so he called Butch to see if Butch could pick him up. Butch said, "Yeah, I'll be glad to pick you up. Be there around 3:00."

"But Bubba," Ed said. "The meeting starts at 5:00. We won't make it in time if we don't leave sooner."

"No problem," Butch said. "I'm flying. We'll have plenty of time."

Ed was leery of flying in a small single-engine plane piloted by the Chairman. "Butch," he said, "are you instrument rated?"

"Naw. Don't need to be on a pretty day like this."

"Well how you gon' know the way to Jackson?" Ed asked.

"Easy," Butch said. "We'll just follow Highway 6 West to Batesville, take a left on I-55 and follow it on in. Do it all the time."

• • •

Robert Clark was the first African-American elected to the Mississippi Legislature since Reconstruction when he took his seat in 1968. At six feet four inches he towered over his colleagues. With a Master's Degree from Michigan State, he was also better educated than most of the white representatives.

A former coach, teacher and school administrator, he was well qualified to serve in the House. Yet no one would sit by him in the House Chamber. During his first days in the House, he sat alone on the far end of the front row. He was ostracized, ignored and made to feel unwanted by most members. This shunning had continued for several weeks in January of 1968 when one day Butch Lambert just ambled across the House floor, as though he were doing nothing out of the ordinary and simply sat down in the vacant seat beside Robert, asking him, "Coach, how's it going?"

This simple act broke many psychological barriers in the Mississippi House of Representatives. It not only made Robert feel welcome, but demonstrated to other members that times were changing. Thereafter Butch and Robert referred to one another as "Coach." They had found a brotherhood of sorts, a common ground. Later in the session, Representative Clark stood at his desk, seeking recognition. He wished to speak on an education bill. The Speaker of the House pretended not to notice Robert, but instead recognized other members, one after the other, to speak on the bill. After about an hour of seeing the white members recognized and still receiving no recognition from the Speaker, Robert began dramatically emptying his desk drawers and packing his documents in a large briefcase. He kicked his chair back, and with much clatter and exaggerated effort, slammed through the Chamber doors and began marching out of the House. He had not gone fifty feet down the hall when he felt someone grab his sleeve. It was Butch.

"What are you doing, Coach?" Butch asked.

"I'm leaving," Robert exclaimed.

"Leaving. Why?" Butch asked.

"What good is it for me to be here? They won't even recognize me to speak! I'm not doing anybody any good here."

"Don't you see Robert . . . this is exactly what they want you to do? They want you to fail!" Butch said. "You are bigger than this, Coach! Now get back in there and do your job. You may be black, but you're a freshman too. And the Speaker doesn't recognize freshmen during their first session."

Robert stayed.

• • •

Butch was always a positive influence in the House and was sorely missed when Governor Winter appointed him to the State Tax Commission. He had a calming influence on others, often defusing tense situations with his wit and kindliness. During my first term in the House, my friend Jerry Wilburn would occasionally "get out of control" on some matter or another. Jerry had a long history in the legislature of creating chaos out of order. Many times I would hear my desk-mate, Charlie Williams or my friend from Inverness, Will Green Poindexter, say, "Ain't nobody can handle Jerry Wilburn since Butch left."

After he became Tax Commissioner, Butch continued to join the boys for breakfast at the big round table in the Sun-N-Sand Resort Hotel where he reported his weekend adventures and commented on the characters he met. One weekend Butch had been to a conference somewhere up North where he had met Jim and Tammy Faye Baker. At the time Jim and Tammy Faye were riding high on the PTL network, spreading their message of faith and prosperity. Though this was well before the Federal Government sent Jim to the pen, I suspect Butch was already on to their game. He recounted that Tammy Faye was "a fairly good lookin' young woman, but she had on so much green eye shadow, I thought her spleen had ruptured!"

• • •

In the Fall of 1984 word went around the capital that "Butch was really going down." He had Lou Gehrig's disease. He had stopped showing up for breakfast at the Sun-N-Sand, and we heard that his old friend from the legislature, Devan Dallas of Pontotoc, was not only assisting him at the Tax Commission, but was now driving him around, pushing his wheelchair and helping Ida every chance he could. Despite his failing health, Butch never dwelt on his disease and continued working until the very end.

One of Butch's childhood friends was long-time Itawamba Junior College head football coach Dudley Miller. When Butch learned of his terminal illness, he told Jerry Wilburn to make sure that Dudley got his Harley-Davidson motorcycle. He said, "I've already told Little Butch and Ida and they know. But I want you to know too just in case there is any talk about it."

Jerry said he would make sure Dudley got the motorcycle. He then asked Butch why he was so concerned that Dudley get it. Butch said, "When we were little boys, our parents couldn't afford to give us bicycles. So we rode stick-horses. My friends and I would race around and around the yard holding our stick-horses in our left hands and slapping our hips and pretending we had horses. Everyone that is but Dudley. Dudley rode his pretend 'motorsickle.' He would straddle it and pretend to kick-start it . . . chuck! chuck! And then he would go 'Vrooooom! Vroooooooom!' And he would hold his hands out in front as though he were grasping the handlebars and he would roar around the yard on his 'motorsickle' and we would follow in his dust on our stick-horses. Dudley always wanted a motorcycle. So you make sure he gets mine." They did.

Folks from all walks of life sought to honor Butch in his last days. The noted self-taught enologist, John Hailman of Oxford, wrote in the *Clarion-Ledger* that the outpouring of affection from around the state, when folks learned of Butch's illness, was "startling." Hailman credited Butch with bringing Mississippi respectability in the wine world through his efforts on the Tax Commission to insure that decisions affecting wine and liquor interests in Mississippi were made by honest and knowledgeable persons. Hailman compared Butch to a true Burgundy, which "is a deep, rich and hearty wine, a cheering companion for all occasions. Old Frenchmen even say that all wine would be Burgundy if it could. If Butch Lambert had been a wine, he would have been a Burgundy, and one of the finest."

Several of Butch's friends, concerned that his health was fading fast, organized a "roast" at the Jackson Coliseum. It was a grand evening. The blind Senator Ellis Bodron, Butch's long-time nemesis in the

Mississippi Senate, was toast-master. Ara Parseghian sent a telegram wishing Butch well, as did Woody Hayes. Dignitaries from the athletic, political and business worlds stood to toast Butch. Walter Payton, the great Chicago Bears running back, captured Butch perfectly, saying simply that "Butch gave his all to humanity." This quote is now on Butch's tombstone.

Dozens of "Butch" stories were told as he sat at the head table, smiling bravely. But he was tiring. About halfway through the dinner, Senator Bodron announced that Butch had to leave because his strength was failing. We stood and applauded as Devan wheeled Butch out of the Coliseum. I thought that I had seen him for the last time. We continued the toasts, like the good soldiers Butch wanted us to be. But he wasn't finished teaching us how to live.

Later that night, around 10:30, John David Pennebaker knocked on my door and said, "Come on. Devan called and said Butch wants to see everyone." The boys of the Sun-N-Sand drifted from their rooms one by one as word spread that Butch wanted to see his buddies, probably for the last time.

We gathered in the little hospitality room and stood quiet and uneasy as Devan rolled Butch's wheelchair into the little room and set up the oxygen tank and adjusted the tube running up his nose. Butch was now tired and gray and could barely whisper, but he wanted to apologize for leaving the roast early. Everyone smiled. And then men started speaking in choking voices as one by one the members told Butch how much they loved him. I don't recall everyone who was present but I know John David Pennebaker, Billy McCoy and my old Delta friend, Jimmy Green were there.

It was a beautiful gathering. Love flowed through the room. Everyone else had spoken when Jerry Wilburn stepped into the middle of the room and said, "Butch, do you remember in 1964 when we was both runnin' for the legislature in Itawamba County. I was runnin' for the Itawamba seat and you was runnin' in that old floater district from Lee and Itawamba?"

Butch nodded and smiled.

"And you remember, we was like a bunch of wrasslers. We'd ride together to the speakin's and then get out and cuss each other on the backs of them ol' flatbed trucks and courthouse steps?"

Butch coughed painfully as he tried to laugh. It was obvious he knew where this tale was going. He still enjoyed a good story and he was being interrogated by a master.

"Butch, you got up there at Tremont and told them people that you was originally from Itawamba County and that you had coached at IJC and that you had married Ida Gilliland from Itawamba County and that if Little Butch got drafted he'd go fight in that war and that when you died you wanted to be buried in Tremont. Do you remember that, Butch?

Butch smiled gently.

"And Butch, the next week we went to Mantachie and you got up on the back of that flat-bed truck and you told them folks that you was originally from Itawamba

County and that you had coached football at IJC and that you had married Ida Gilliland from Itawamba County and that if Little Butch got drafted, he'd go fight in that war and that you had kin folks in Mantachie and that when you died you wanted to be buried in Mantachie. You remember that, Butch?"

Butch grinned sheepishly.

"Then we went to Fulton, Butch. And you got up there on the Courthouse steps and told them people that you was a graduate of Itawamba Agricultural High School where you said you had played football and basketball and baseball and that you had coached at IJC and that you had married Ida Gilliland, your high school sweetheart from Fulton, Mississippi, and that if Little Butch got drafted, he'd go off and fight in that war and that when you died you wanted to be buried in Fulton. Ain't that what you said, Butch?"

Butch smiled again.

"And Butch, I called your hand on it at Fulton. I got up there and told them people at Fulton what you had said to them people in Tremont and Mantachie. I asked you to tell them which group you was lyin' to. Where were you really gonna be buried? Fulton or Mantachie or Tremont? You remember that, Butch?"

Butch grinned.

Wilburn became very serious. "Butch, we know you ain't got long. Now you done lied to some of them folks. Either the folks at Fulton or Mantachie or Tremont. And we need to know now. We cain't go 'round digging you back up and reburying you ever six or seven days.

What would Little Butch and Scotty and Vicki and Amy think. Now which one is it gonna be?"

Butch smiled again. We leaned forward to hear how he was going to get himself out of this predicament. It looked tough. Then he softly whispered, "Jerry . . . do you remember . . . what I told you at Fulton . . . when you called me a liar?"

Jerry smiled back and nodded.

Butch looked at all of us and whispered with a sweet smile, "Well, I'll tell you the same thing tonight. *Let Ida decide. . . .*"

Peace filled the room. Within days the Mississippi Flag was flying at half-mast as Butch's body lay in state in the Capitol rotunda where thousands lined the corridors and halls to pay their last respects to one of Mississippi's finest.

Another Gentleman from Itawamba

Edwin J. "Jerry" Wilburn of Mantachie, Mississippi is a chief source of delight in my existence. For more than three decades, Jerry has played many roles in my life. He has been a good friend. An erratic, though sometimes brilliant, mentor. A valued, if frustrating client. A part-time colleague. And a painfully honest critic. He is as loyal as the Queen's guard when others criticize me but can be a real 'cross-eyed bear' when he and I differ.

When the mood strikes, Jerry Wilburn can charm Satan out of his pitchfork. On the other hand, he can also 'worry the horns off a billy-goat' as we like to say in North Mississippi. His natural charm, combined with a healthy dose of big ol' square-headed country stubbornness, make Jerry Wilburn one of the most colorful individuals I have ever known. He cannot be limited to one age. He would be his own unique self in any century.

I first met Jerry in 1968 when he selected me, at the age of 12, to be his page for a week. It was my first trip to Jackson and of course I was seduced by the grand beauty of the beaux art style of the Mississippi Capitol building. I have seen some of the world beyond Jackson since 1968. I like to think that I now have a bit more perspective about people and places and things than I had as a twelve-year-old boy. I have seen the Eiffel Tower and I have strolled through Westminster Abbey. I have slept in Bruges and dined in Tremont. I have visited several state parks and I have seen the world's largest ball of twine. Yet few structures rival our Mississippi Capitol for pure elegance, even if it was paid for by the Illinois Central Railroad. The marbled hallways and stained glass ceilings; the Italianate trim and rich murals; the portraits of old governors; the ornate elevators: all besotted me, in 1968, with a drunken sense of history. And power. Like most young folks who spend a week paging in the capital, I really couldn't see how the government could function when my week of racing up and down four flights of marbled stairs running errands for legislators and eagerly doing the work of the people had ended. Thus was born my dream that I too might some day be a legislator. Just like Mr. Wilburn. And as surely as night follows day, I found myself representing Itawamba County in 1984, alongside the Honorable Edwin J. "Jerry" Wilburn. I ain't been the same since.

From my current perch on the Federal bench, I enjoy watching lawyers and witnesses and jurors and court personnel as we all go about our respective duties. I have long been fascinated with how personalities develop and what makes a person unique and interesting. Unfortunately, many people never overcome the circumstances and place of their birth. Some, polished by privilege, are rather tiresome to be around. Others, perhaps born with less opportunity, but blessed with more varied life experiences, often exhibit quicker wit and broader humanity. I am always alert for that delightful spark of originality laying dormant within each of us. That phrase or expression which says, "This is the real me." Some folk never let those moments come to light. They hide their lights under bushel baskets, afraid for the world to see their individuality. Not Jerry. Jerry Wilburn is the real deal in every word he utters. He is a strong personality. And, to the surprise of many, he is also one of the most successful businessmen in Mississippi.

Jerry didn't make it to the top by climbing the traditional rungs of respectability. His résumé boasts few academic degrees. Jerry Wilburn made his mark by trusting his keen insight into human nature. He understands his fellow man (and woman). He knows by instinct how to motivate or frustrate, entertain or infuriate others. He is a natural.

Wilburn masks a profound grasp of human nature with an adroit use of ancient "rhetorical devices." Of course he doesn't know this. And neither did I until I ran across some old dialogues by a fellow named Socrates. I didn't learn about these devices in my studies at Itawamba Agricultural High School and I suspect you may not have heard of these debating tools either, so a bit of classical history may be helpful here.

There was a gang of old Greek philosophers known as the "Sophists" who believed in using certain rhetorical devices to win arguments. Now Jerry Wilburn has never heard of the Sophists, nor had they heard of him. Yet Jerry and the Sophists have much in common. Primarily, the Sophists, like Mr. Wilburn, sought to win their arguments without regard for truth. The point was to win.

Later thinkers who studied the Sophists, like Socrates and Aristotle, identified certain tricks the Sophists used to win arguments. These rhetorical devices include the use of hyperbole; archaism; exaggeration; malapropism; euphemism, et cetera. My long observation of Mr. Wilburn convinces me that he is a master, by instinct, of the same rhetorical devices that the ancient Greeks spent their lives learning. Let me give you a few examples.

Mr. Wilburn is a genius at using *malapropisms.* Now I know that malapropism is a mighty big word for me to be throwing around. I do not use it here to impress you. And I don't mean to imply that it is such a word as Mr. Wilburn might use. In fact, I don't believe I have ever heard him say anything close to malapropism. (It would be fun to hear him try.) Malapropisms to Jerry Wilburn are like electrical currents to me. I don't understand how they work, but I know how to switch on a light. Same way with Mr. Wilburn and malapropisms.

I think malapropism means using the wrong word in the right place. Or vice versa. I'm not sure which. But maybe it makes no difference. Anyway that's how Jerry Wilburn uses malapropisms. With stunning effect. Let me share with you a few examples of a master of malapropisms.

When I'm Dead, and When I'm Gone

This author excepted, another outstanding Wilburn protege in the Mississippi House of Representatives is the Honorable Steve Holland from Plantersville. Back in the early 80's, when Steve and I first took office, Mr. Wilburn insisted on chauffeuring us to and from Jackson. Each Monday morning he would first rendezvous with Steve in Plantersville and then drive to Aberdeen, where he and Steve would drag me from my second floor law office overlooking Commerce Street, and the three of us would head toward Jackson, all scrunched-up in Jerry's red Ford pickup. (This was before Jerry got rich and started driving the four-door pickups he favors today.)

Our weekly Jackson pilgrimage soon took on a life of its own. Holland is sometimes as colorful and entertaining as Wilburn, and both can be outright audacious when least expected. (I guess the surprise factor is what makes audacity audacious. It happens when you least expect it.)

Steve Holland is a farmer, a philosopher, a gifted

pianist and a faux rustique. He is also a licensed mortician. Back in 1984, Steve had offered me a fine marble urn that someone had left as a sample at his funeral home. I had earlier mentioned that I wanted to be cremated when I died, based upon some romantic notion I had at the time about not taking up any more space than necessary once my spirit departed its earthly home. Holland promised me a marble urn which he wanted to get rid of anyway since he wasn't in favor of cremation. (No need to sell those high-dollar caskets if folks are going to be roasted rather than rotted. Did you know that in Mississippi you have to be embalmed before you are cremated? Doesn't make sense to anybody but morticians. But that's another story for another day. And it ain't likely to change with Steve in the legislature.)

Holland was to deliver my urn one Monday morning when he and Wilburn arrived in Aberdeen. I was excited for their arrival and hurried down the stairs to meet my colleagues when I heard Representative Wilburn's familiar honk. I immediately asked Steve "Where's my vase?" That is what I called it. A vase.

Steve replied that he had forgotten it but would bring it next week. I was disappointed but let the matter pass.

The next Monday, Jerry and Steve showed up again. As we headed toward the Trace, I asked about my vase. Steve said he wasn't sure that he could give it to me. I replied that a promise was a promise. I felt, after all I had done for him, that he ought to come through on such a small favor. He replied that he had "done all he could." I knew this to be a non-answer. Some might even say his response was evasive.

On to his ploy, I asked Representative Holland directly, "So just where is my vase that you promised me?"

To which he replied, "Dadgum it, Mills. I gave it to a history teacher at Plantersville Elementary School."

"What for?" I asked. "Did you tell them it was an old Roman relic or somethin'?"

"I told 'em it was a flower pot."

"Well, maybe they'll name the school after you some day," I said. "For all you've done for them."

Our spat continued several miles down the Trace, the tension rising milepost by milepost, as I continued to indict Mr. Holland's ability to keep his word. After about 20 minutes of this, Mr. Wilburn slowed the pickup, pulled it onto the shoulder, jerked the transmission into park and said "Lord God, Holland! Why don't you just go out and buy Little Mills another *urinal*?"

That, dear reader, is a *malapropism*. Here are some more:

Law and Order

Jerry Wilburn once killed an Appropriations Bill providing for more Highway Patrol officers by making an impassioned speech on the floor of the House in favor of citizens' rights under the U.S. Constitution. He concluded his remarks with the statement that we had "all the law we can stand now and we don't need no more Highway *Control*." How do you respond to that?

The Art of Oratin'

Jerry was instrumental, in his capacity as Chairman of the Local and Private Committee, in obtaining State funding for a building for the Mississippi Chapter of the Daughters of the American Revolution. The good ladies wished to reward Chairman Wilburn for his efforts on their behalf so they invited him to speak at their annual convention. He made a good talk about motherhood and "the hand that rocks the cradle" and who can find a virtuous woman and such. They ate it up. He finally concluded his remarks, and the fine matrons stood and clapped their hands and cheered wildly. It was a touching moment for all concerned. When the applause finally subsided, Jerry leaned into the microphone, and brushing back tears, thanked the ladies for "giving me my first standing *ovulation*."

A Rose By Any Other Name

We had one old fellow in the Legislature who looked like he had been serving since the Civil War. (He voted that way too.) Out of respect for the dead, and to keep from getting sued, I will call him Representative Boregard. Representative Boregard, aged and feeble, lived only to serve in the Mississippi House of Representatives. He was nearly blind, could hardly walk, and was moderately senile. Of course, this did not disqualify him from holding public office.

Supposedly, in better times, he had been quite a lady's man.

Deadline days were very hard on Representative Boregard since these sessions would often last late into the night. Yet he never complained. He just loved pushing those green buttons. As he said, "I always support the committee." And he did. That meant he voted for every bill reported out of every committee. Regardless of merit. And against all amendments. Even those which made good sense.

One deadline night the boys in the House had been particularly cantankerous. The House failed to adjourn in a timely fashion at five o'clock. So we just kept working. About nine in the evening, the Speaker tried to get the House to adjourn again. No luck. So we kept right on working and Representative Boregard just kept hitting that green button, like the gallant young Pelham pumping his cannon at Fredericksburg. The Chairmen kept calling up bills and we kept debating and voting. After another hour or so, Representative Boregard collapsed at his desk, coughing and wheezing. He was gray-faced. Some thought he was having the big one. But he wouldn't leave his post. He just kept on punching that green button.

The boys called for our legislative nurse, who knew just what to do. Within minutes, the nurse and the doctor of the day (a little something the medical association does for the legislature) had installed a clear plastic tent around Representative Boregard. They told the courtly Charlie Capps from Bolivar County to put out his cigar and began pumping pure oxygen into the tent. Representative Boregard seemed to revive. Though he couldn't hear a thing going on inside his clear tent, the good man sat and coughed and continued to vote.

Mr. Wilburn and I were standing in back of the Chamber observing this pyrrhic dedication to duty when Jerry said, "Look-a-there Little Mills. That's what 50 years in the Legislature will do for you. If you keep hangin' around with all them lobbyists and drinkin' their whiskey and smokin' their cigars, you're gonna end up just like that. That *Noczema* is gonna kill him yet."

Larger Than Life

Hyperbole is the use of exaggeration for argumentative effect. The ancient Greeks were fond of hyperbole, not only as a rhetorical device, but also in their poetry and literature. They had nothing on Mr. Wilburn. Here is hyperbole at its best.

The years have been kind to Representative Holland. He and I were both rather trim young fellows when first elected to the Mississippi Legislature in 1984. The beloved late Senator John Stennis often observed that "some folks swell and some folks grow" when elected to public office. A few rare souls do both. Over twenty years of prosperity and easy living in Jackson have somewhat expanded Steve's girth. On the other hand, his profound knowledge of law and keen grasp of all pending legislative issues has also expanded, "commensurate therewith" as we lawyers like to say. Consequently, Steve's frequent opinions and studious pronouncements are often featured in the papers. He also waxes eloquent on Channel 9 News out of Tupelo, about this, that and the other. In truth, he has become a real media favorite. Jerry Wilburn told me that he saw Representative Holland on TV the other day, talking about the "bottom line." According to Wilburn, "That boy has got so big that I had to get another TV and push 'em together so I could get 'im all on the screen!"

Billy Bowles listening to Steve Holland give Jerry Wilburn the "Bottom Line"

Pending Business

The Sophists understood *irony*, which rhetorically is the expression of something contrary to its intended meaning. Watch Mr. Wilburn turn a phrase around, ironically.

Mississippi legislators are often requested to assist constituents. They may be asked to help a wayward son-in-law find a job with the Game and Fish Commission; or help a County Supervisor's niece get a job teaching school, even if she can't pass the state teacher's examination; or be called upon to preach a funeral now and then. It all comes with the territory.

Representatives Butch Lambert and Jerry Wilburn were contacted by the patriarch of a prominent Northeast Mississippi family seeking help with a legal problem. It seems that the man's son had a criminal case pending before one of our Circuit Judges in Tupelo, and the family had found no luck convincing the good judge to go along with a light sentence for the young miscreant. The father asked Butch and Jerry if they could "help out with the judge." Of course neither of them were lawyers, but that didn't stop them from giving advice and assisting where they could. Butch and Jerry said they would be glad to "see what we can do."

Jerry and Butch went to see the judge and dutifully sat in the hallway outside his chambers, waiting their turn with patience. Soon enough they were allowed in. The judge received them with good humor and tactfully paid them such deference as their stations in life deserved. However, as soon as Butch and Jerry began explaining the purpose of their trip, the good judge stopped them. "I'm sorry, gentlemen," he said. "But I can't talk to you about that matter. It would be unethical. That is pending business." He sent them away disappointed.

A year after the Butch and Jerry visit with the Judge in Tupelo, a judges' pay increase bill came before the legislature. Jerry Wilburn didn't need much encouragement to oppose a pay raise for anybody. However, he was particularly opposed to giving judges a raise. He made a speech on the floor of the House talking about how seldom judges actually worked and argued that the money would be better used if given to the "pore." The legislation was in serious trouble.

Word of Mr. Wilburn's antics and efforts to kill the judge's pay increase bill spread quickly among the judiciary. The State's judges caucused over who they could send to Jackson to "take care of Jerry Wilburn." No one was eager for the task. Finally, the other judges prevailed upon the good judge from Tupelo to go to Jackson and "talk to Jerry" about the pay bill. The judge did as requested and drove down to Jackson to see Mr. Wilburn, who was holding forth on the virtues and vices of various bills before the Local and Private Committee which he chaired. Jerry allowed the judge to wait a time with patience, then received him cordially, with all due deference, of course. After some brief small talk about the weather and such, the judge cut to the chase.

"Jerry," he said, "I need to talk to you about that pay bill for judges you've been speaking against."
Whoa! Jerry cut him off immediately. "Judge, I'm sorry. I cain't talk to you about that right now. It'd be unethical. That's *pending business!*"

A History Lesson

The ancient Greeks identified *metonymy* as the substitution of one word for another which it may suggest. Watch for Mr. Wilburn's use of metonymy in this anecdote. There is some good *hyperbole* here too.

The ubiquitous Cooperative Extension Service is a well-fed sacred cow in Mississippi. This service helps preserve our rural heritage by furnishing every county in the State with at least one County Agent and usually a couple of Assistant County Agents, all driving State furnished green pickup trucks, and a Home Economics lady, whether the county needs them or not. The Service also sponsors rural "Home-makers" clubs and 4-H Clubs and various other relics from our subsistence economy past. More important, the Service supplies legislators and state officials, from the governor down to the secretary of state, with free Mississippi State cheese at Christmas and free tomato plants just before Easter. (Just because a fellow gets free cheese for four years does not mean he's entitled to get it forever. The Service has standards. Should the voters throw a rascal out of office, the Service directors, mimicking Dickens' knitress, Madame Defarge, remove the name of said rascal from the free cheese list. This I know to be true.)

Jerry Wilburn, as Butch Lambert said, "got red-shirted" by the voters of Itawamba County from 1980 to 1984. (Remarkably, these were four of the most progressive years the Mississippi Legislature experienced in the 20th Century. Perhaps the planets were properly aligned, or maybe this phenomenon can best be explained by Wilburn's absence from the Capitol.) In true bureaucratic fashion, the Service Agriculturalists purged Mr. Wilburn's name from the free cheese list in 1980. It was as though he had never existed. But wait! The voters of Itawamba County rehabilitated Mr. Wilburn by sending him back to Jackson in 1984. Alas, the Agriculturalists had to put him back on the list. And so began their troubles.

Mr. Wilburn is slow to forgive and never forgets. He made it his mission in 1985 to shut down the Cooperative Extension Service. He commenced his battle on the floor of the House of Representatives in January of 1985 by offering an amendment to cut in half the Appropriations Bill providing funding for the Service. Jerry began his formal remarks by launching into an immediate harangue against County Agents, 4-H Clubs, Experiment Stations and other arms of the Cooperative Extension Service.

The members cheered Wilburn on as he preached and ranted against waste in government. He reminded his audience that the county agents had introduced kudzu to Mississippi in the 1930's. And he told us that under the Roosevelt Administration the Cooperative Extension Service had also brought the first beavers to Mississippi so the "pore little hill-county farmers" would have a winter "cash-crop" capturing the little four-footed fur-bearing creatures. He even told his listeners about a study at Mississippi State, home of the Cooperative Extension Service, to document the breeding habits of bobcats, so more of them could be released to help control the beaver population. He challenged the members to "just imagine what them bobcats will do to the turkeys and quail!"

The members cheered wildly as Mr. Wilburn defended good sense and lambasted waste in government. In their hearts, they knew he was right. Finally his time expired. The Speaker called for a vote. Lordy, Lordy! By a unanimous, thundering "voice" vote, Mr. Wilburn's amendment carried unanimously. These sacred cows of state government had finally been corralled! The Cooperative Extension Service Budget had been cut in half!

Mr. Wilburn's victory was short-lived. A small number of members then sheepishly stood at their desks, demanding a "roll call" vote. You could always count on a certain dozen or so members to stand and call for a recorded vote whenever a real tough issue was before the House. These malcontents demanded a roll call whenever they sensed an opportunity to embarrass other house members. They usually exercised this power on votes dealing with legislative pay raises, open meetings laws and the so-called "lobbyist reform" acts. (I usually voted against lobbyist reform. I don't believe you can reform lobbyists. Better to just outlaw the rascals). The standing demand for a roll call required the members to "go on the board," thereby making a record of their votes on the amendment by pushing the yes or no button and lighting up the voting board hanging above the House Chamber . "Yes" votes are green and "No" votes are red. Of course you don't have to vote "on the board" consistent with your voice vote. The Speaker at the time, Buddie Newman, counted the members standing before their colleagues, then said "Open the machine, Mr. Clerk." The same members who only moments before had energetically and loudly voted *vive voce* for Mr. Wilburn's amendment now sheepishly turned on their leader. Bright red "No" buttons lit up the board.

Mr. Wilburn, stood alone at the podium, watching his hard-fought victory collapse as the bloodred "No" votes outshined the green "Yes" votes, 115 to 7. He glared at his shame-faced colleagues and remarked, with sad resignation, "Now I know how General *Cluster* felt when he looked up and seen all them Indians!"

The story does not end here. I voted with Mr. Wilburn all the way on his Cooperative Extension Service amendment. I admired his pluck. Consequently, I too soon absorbed a full assault from the invidious Service forces.

On the day after my vote for Mr. Wilburn's amendment, I received a telephone call from my dear Grandma Dulaney who had recently won a blue ribbon in the Clay Community Homemakers Club for best canned fig preserves. It seems someone had told her that she couldn't go to Jackson for the state-wide competition for best canned fig preserves because her grandson had voted to cut off the gas money for the Cooperative Extension Service van. In other words, because of Representative Mills, the old folks of Itawamba County wouldn't be able to go to the State meeting. What could I say to Grandma?

Two days later I received an invitation from the Lick Skillet Homemakers Club, inviting me to speak at their annual meeting. The invitation said it was a "pot-luck supper" and to "bring your ASS cause we intend to eat it out!" I declined the invitation.

The Cooperative Extension Service folks are, thankfully, forgiving spirits. I continued to receive my free cheese and tomato plants until 1995 when Governor Fordice appointed me to the Supreme Court. Alas, for some reason, they don't give free cheese and tomato plants to judges. I should have known.

I Wanna Go Home

Archaism is the use of an old or obsolete form for another. Mr. Wilburn often mixes archaism, metonymy and malapropisms all in one phrase.

I remember one session in the early 80's when neither the House nor the Senate could muster the votes to go home *sine die,* which is a Latin term meaning *without any future date.* (If you look it up in your *Webster's*

Dictionary, you may note that Mississippi's Hodding Carter is credited with correct usage of the term.) In legislative parlance, the words mean the last day of the session. In order to go home, the legislature must adopt a *sine die* resolution. It was in the middle of the Allain administration and the State was broke. School teachers were threatening a strike, tax collections were slowing to a dribble, folks were getting laid off from their jobs left and right and there was just a general feeling of irritation with the legislature throughout the land, as though we had caused the pain. From a distance, that view had merit. The House wouldn't pass the Senate bills and the Senate wouldn't pass the House bills and the Governor was vetoing everybody's bills. We were in a mess. The newspapers were fussing about the legislature continuing in session and pundits were making their usual tiresome rant to "make 'em serve without pay." The legislature cannot finally adjourn and go home without passing a sine die resolution.

It was in late spring, as I recall, when Mr. Wilburn joined me by the Sun-N-Sand pool late one afternoon. I know it was late in the spring because little tadpoles had already hatched in the green swimming pool water. Mr. Wilburn said, "Well Little Mills, they've sent an ambulance to get us."

I said, "What?"

"I said, Little Mills, the folks in Itawamba County has sent a ambulance to get us."

"What do you mean," I asked. "Why would they send an ambulance to get us?"

"They read in that *Tupelo Daily Journal* that Norma Fields said it was time for the Legislature to *sign or die* and they knew me and you wouldn't sign!"

The Sting

And of course Mr. Wilburn, like all great rhetoricians, is not above using a bit of *exaggeration,* which the uninformed might mistake for plain untruths. See if you can tell the difference.

Representative Wilburn often disagreed with my votes on particular legislation. He was not shy about commenting on what the "folks back home" would do to me come election time. I remember one Monday afternoon when Jerry said "Lord, Little Mills, folks is hot, folks is hot."

"What are they hot about, Jerry?"

"Lord God, they're hot about your vote on that Game and Fish bill layst week. I was at Clyde Christian's grocery this mornin', and Lord God, folks is hot."

I feigned indifference to what the folks back home thought of my vote on a Game and Fish bill. But the folks at Clyde Christian's had always been mighty kind to me and I hoped I hadn't offended them. I couldn't wait to get back to Aberdeen Friday afternoon, check my messages at the office, jump back in the car and then drive anther hour to Peppertown, so I could casually pull up in front of Clyde Christian's Grocery and buy a tank of gas. This I did. I was filling it up when David Bean, Clyde's son-in-law, came out to pass the time. After exchanging a few country pleasantries about the weather and such with David, I inquired, "David, are folks very upset about my vote on that Game and Fish bill last week"?

David looked at me and said, "No, I haven't heard a word about it. Except for Jerry Wilburn. He was by here a week ago raising Cain about it."

Ain't he special?

Farm Policy

I am unable to find a Greek identification for the following device, which I classify as an original *Wilburnism*. As you can see by now, Mr. Wilburn is as gifted with words as Rembrandt was with a paintbrush. And all the world is Mr. Wilburn's palette.

Mississippi farmers have long dealt with hellish weather and low commodity prices. Since the 1930's they have also had to contend with kudzu and beavers. The worst was yet to come. In the late 1960's a family of fire ants from Guatemala disembarked from a banana boat in Gulfport and settled on the Mississippi Gulf Coast. They quickly adapted to our climate and by the early 1970's had spread across the State. Fire ants became the most dangerous threat to Mississippi farmers since the boll weevil first appeared in the 19th Century. But boll weevils bite only cotton bolls. A fire-ant sting can be deadly.

All things agricultural eventually become political in Mississippi. Soon enough the State Department of

Agriculture, headed by the legendary Jim Buck Ross, got in the business of fighting fire ants with a powerful chemical known as Mirex. Jim Buck was known for always getting his way in the Mississippi legislature. (He also gained some national notoriety for his famous biscuit conversation with Vice-Presidential candidate Geraldine Ferraro). Jim Buck had employees scattered across the State in close competition, numerically, with the Cooperative Extension Service. Jim Buck's folks are also supposed to help the farmer. These folks were a powerful political force in local politics and were presciently treated by the legislature with the respect one owes a rattlesnake. You didn't want Jim Buck's boys holding a fish fry in your district unless you were invited.

Jim Buck convinced the State Legislature to pay for a Mirex chemical plant to be run by the Department of Agriculture. Mirex was deadly in getting rid of fireants. Over time we learned that it was also effective in eradicating birds, fish and small children. There was some proof that it might also be a carcinogen. Over much protest from the State Agriculture Department, and much jabber about our sovereign state's right to poison who we want to poison, the Federal Government finally banned its use.

Mirex having been outlawed, someone introduced a bill to appropriate funds to the Department of Agriculture to allow Jim Buck Ross to continue a governmental study to find new ways to get rid of the dreaded fire-ants. As I said, Jim Buck Ross usually got what he wanted from the Mississippi Legislature. He didn't expect opposition on this bill.

The fire ant bill came up for debate. Mr. Wilburn, true to his conservative instincts, and in direct opposition to his best political interests, spoke against spending any more money to study the fire-ant problem. He suggested instead, ". . . that we send all Jim Buck's employees up to the Tennessee State line and line 'em up from Arkansas to Alabama and *march 'em South like Sherman to the Gulf Coast and they can just stomp all them far-aints out.*"

When Heaven and Earth Pass

Kelly Wade Prestage springs into mind as far back as I can recall. I remember sitting on the porch steps of our little house in the Ryan's Well community, far north of Fulton, going through my mother's high school annual, *The Mirror*. There is a picture of this big burly-looking fellow, with black curly hair and a dark complexion, grinning mischievously at the camera, decked out in an Itawamba Indians football uniform, cocking his arm with a football as though he wanted to throw it at me. I thought that fellow was scary looking.

One Sunday afternoon soon after our move to Fulton, my family went to a Fulton Volunteer Fire Department fish fry being held to finance the purchase of a new, used red fire-truck. One of the fellows I saw at the fire station, jumping about and laughing, was the big burly fellow from my mother's annual. That is the first time I recall seeing Kelly Wade Prestage.

A year or two later, Kelly helped start our first annual Fulton Grammar School Halloween Carnival to raise money to buy air conditioners for the classrooms. He was laughing and calling everybody "Baby" or "Brother" and filling popcorn bags for the children. I was quick enough then to know this was a special person, though I couldn't have told you his name. He simply had a big happy presence which made you want to smile. This was his gift.

Kelly Wade and his brother-in-law, James Chatham, started C&P Auto Parts in Fulton in the late 1950s. Back in my high school days, I spent many Saturday mornings replacing parts on my old '65 Mustang, just to keep it running. A highlight of these repair jobs was going to C&P Auto Parts to buy a fan belt or a battery or a screwdriver, and be entertained to boot. It was a real delight to be greeted by Kelly Wade standing behind the counter in blue jeans and a faded blue shirt, his back half-turned to the customers, eyebrows raised, saying "Hey, Brother" to the next customer in line. I would tell him my problem, he would diagnose the condition, and if he wasn't too rushed, help make the repairs in the parking lot.

As a boy, I was a member of Boy Scout Troop 32, sponsored by the Fulton Methodist Church. Our Scout Master, Billy Bonds McElroy, took us to Camp Yocona every summer. Most of us didn't have the money for camp tuition, so Kelly Wade and other church men would bake chickens on Saturday mornings for us to sell to raise funds for Scout camp. It was at one of these cookings that I first remember being spoken to by Kelly

Wade. Billy Bonds, or B. B. as everyone called him, designated me as some sort of Troop Leader to organize the other boys to help

Kelly Wade cooked the chickens. He already had the big hickory pit smoking when we got there. Being boys, we were more interested in playing tackle-tag in the park behind the church than cooking chickens. However, being Troop Leader, I felt obliged to hang around near the fire and at least look interested in what Kelly Wade was doing. I remember awkwardly dodging from side to side as Kelly Wade rushed back and forth, wrapping chicken quarters in tin foil or chunking more hickory in the fire. I must have been getting on his nerves. For the first thing I remember Kelly Wade Prestage saying to me as a person was "Son, if you're gonna stand around, stand in a strain!" I got the message. I got busy! Kelly Wade had no use for slackers.

Kelly Wade Prestage and some of the Boys

To Kelly Wade, everyone started out as "Brother." But if he really liked you, he called you "Baby." Though he didn't spend a lot of time fretting about the human condition, his affection for others represented his sense that we are all in this together. The term "Baby" also tells us a bit about small-town Mississippi. I know where it came from. Kelly Wade picked it up from L.C. Stone, one of our fine old black friends who helped rear Kelly Wade and about half the white boys in Fulton. He helped rear me too. And everyone was Baby to L.C. The best small town traditions never die. (Kelly Wade had a third category of folks whom he referred to as "shoe clerks." These were the folks who hung around him to see what would happen next. I was often in this category.

Mona and I moved to Aberdeen in 1980 when I finished law school. Our first home there was a big one. The two-story beauty, built in the 1880's, was so large it had its own name, "The Oaks." We were proud to own such a house. (We didn't have many such houses in Itawamba County when I was growing up. The only house I recall having its own name when I was growing up was "the Pore-House.") We were in "The Oaks" only a few months when we invited our Fulton friends, Johnny and Bessie Lynn Crane and Kelly Wade and the love of his life, Linda, to Aberdeen so we could show off our new surroundings. I cooked steaks and Mona baked potatoes and everyone declared dinner a success. Since we had spent what little money we had on a down payment for the house, we didn't have much in the way of furniture. Our guests kindly declined comment on the lawn chairs in the dining room. But they must have noticed our lack of fancy furnishings, for a week or two later Kelly Wade showed up in Aberdeen with a beautiful antique Victrola in the back of his old brown Chevy pickup. He also had a fine collection of ancient heavy John Phillip Sousa albums. These are the best kinds of gifts. Unexpected.

Kelly and I shared a love for music. I like to listen to it. He loved to perform. He wasn't a polished singer, yet he was always eager to light up a gathering with his version of a Hank Williams classic or Blueberry Hills by Fats Domino. Good lyrics easily moved him to tears. And he loved to dance, though neither was he the best dancer I have ever seen. In my bookcase you will find three little smiling ceramic figures reflecting our mutual love of music: a collection of jazz players. One plucks a bass fiddle. Another pounds a piano. The third blows a horn. Kelly Wade said he saw them at a flea market in Waterloo, Alabama, and they reminded him of me. More gifts.

Several of Kelly's shoe clerks and I were building our own cabin down on the Tombigbee River a few years ago. Kelly heard of the project and showed up with three old straw-backed, metal bar stools. The seats were about five feet above floor level (dangerous), the back was out of one, another had a bent leg, and the third was barely serviceable. Though we didn't have a bar in the cabin, we thanked him richly for the gifts because he seemed so proud of his contribution. We later found they worked fairly well in the deer stands after Kelly's nephew, the ever-resourceful Brad Chatham, cut the stool legs off. Kelly's childhood friend, Don Holcomb is fond of saying that Kelly Wade would give you not only the shirt off his back and his last dollar but he would then go borrow another five if he thought you needed it.

Generosity of spirit.

On December 1, 1995, Kelly Wade learned that I was having a party that night at my house to celebrate my investiture as a justice on the Mississippi Supreme Court. He was concerned that Mona and I might not be able to put on a good show without some help. By noon, he had taken charge of the event. He made signs to direct traffic from Itawamba Community College to my house. He furnished shoe clerks to park cars. He donated three hundred pounds of ice, swept off the front porch, cut the grass, and, late in the afternoon, asked if there was anything else I needed done. I knew he was worn out. I just said, "Naw, baby. Go home, get cleaned up and make sure you bring Miss Linda tonight."

That night our home filled with neighbors and friends and preachers and politicians, several judges and a few reprobates and other assorted courtesans from our circle of relations. Most of the more refined folks stayed in the front rooms, politely gossiping of the weather and politics and such, but the hard-core faithful knew the action was in the back in my "study," where I was entertaining the boys with old recordings of Elmore James and Jimmy Rogers and Willie and Waylon. We were having our own good time, Kelly Wade included, when I saw Linda politely peep into the room, probably to keep an eye on Kelly. About that time, I slipped an old Ben E. King tune into the CD player and Kelly spied Linda and these classic words filled the room:

> *When the night is cold . . .*
> *and the land is dark . . .*
> *and the moon . . .*
> *is the only light you see . . .*

Kelly pulled her into the room, saying, "Come on Shorty, we gotta dance." (He always called her Shorty.) She gave us her special twinkling smile and they lit up the room doing an old '50s waltz. . .

> *no I won't be afraid . . .*
> *no I won't be afraid . . .*
> *just as long . . .*
> *as you stand . . .*
> *stand by me . . .*

We knew we were living.

Though Kelly sang in the church choir, and just loved being in the singing Christmas Tree, he wasn't a big fan of Wednesday night choir practice. To his credit, he was happy to manage the food pantry for needy families at the Methodist Church, feed the preachers when necessary, help keep up the church grounds and generally serve wherever needed. But Wednesday nights were reserved for a special fellowship. Kelly Wade was founder of the Itawamba County Wednesday Night Brotherhood meeting, a shifting assortment of Kelly's "boys" whom he classed as "shoe clerks" or "ribbon salesmen" or "pea pickers" and who enjoyed the weekly gathering at various cabins around the county where they cooked, told tall tales, confessed their sins to like-minded listeners, and now and then committed a few minor indiscretions. His "cookin's" offered a revival of the secular spirit where a fellow could enjoy refreshments and rest from his labors. Kelly Wade was the boss at these events, though his rule was sometimes challenged by two of his chief partners in mischief, Brother Johnny Crane and Deacon Jerry Wilburn.

Kelly Wade's health began declining in the 1980's, when he had the first of several life-saving heart surgeries. All the boys in the Brotherhood fretted over Kelly Wade after the first surgery. He missed a few Wednesday night services, but after a short convalescence, showed up one night with his big, wide broken-mouthed grin and new pig valves attached to his heart. Of course everyone wanted to hear about his surgery and subsequent recuperation. He had lost some weight and seemed tired but was otherwise in high spirits. When asked about the procedures he had undergone, he said "Aw, baby, there ain't nothin' to it. I feel like a million dollars now. The only problem I got is a cravin' for shelled corn. Gotta feed these shoats, you know!"

These are some of the thoughts that passed through my mind in September of 2002 when my neighbor Larry Montgomery, pulled into my driveway and said simply, "Kelly Wade is dead."

The Fulton United Methodist Church is blessed with at least four licensed, ordained Methodist ministers among its membership. I have also noticed one or two regularly attending preachers and priests from other faiths. Consequently, we can't have a good funeral or memorial service at the Fulton United Methodist Church without hearing from a passel of preachers. Just wouldn't feel right to leave one of 'em out. Fortunately, being Methodists, the four of them combined can usually pack it all in in under sixty minutes. They don't get too tiresome that way. And they did a fine job for Kelly Wade.

Brother Ray Stokes and his colleagues, the Reverend Glyn Wiygul, Dr. Roy McAlilly, the Reverend James Price and Kelly Wade's childhood friend, Don Holcomb, made the service very special. Eddie Moore's solo rendition of *The Dance* by Garth Brooks brought tears to the toughest eyes. But the person who made this memorial service really special was Kelly Wade Prestage himself. We knew we were celebrating his last dance.

Brother Wiygul challenged us to speak often of Kelly Wade and to write down our memories. I accept Brother Wiygul's challenge, with the sure knowledge that others much closer to Kelly likely have even more to say.

Don Holcomb reminded us of a young Kelly Wade riding his little wooden wagon in Fulton in the 1940's, the wagon pulled by a little black and white Shetland Pony as Kelly cheerfully delivered sweet milk every morning before school. And he talked of how Kelly had a mid-life mission of cutting wood for anybody in the county who had a wood-burning stove. Kelly couldn't rest if you had a wood-burning stove until you had at least a cord of wood stacked for the winter. It just had to be done. Free of charge, of course. With a lot of laughs along the way. Mr. Holcomb's anecdotes nailed some key attributes of Kelly Wade Prestage. Work and laughter. A lot of both.

Dr. McAlilly reminded us that Kelly Wade was dozing in the choir one Sunday morning a few years ago when the preacher called on Brother Johnny Crane to give a church financial report. Kelly Wade waked with a start when he heard Johnny's name called and spied his bosom friend "walking the aisle." As Johnny approached the confessional, Kelly Wade blurted in his rich Itawamba baritone the plaintive admonition, "Don't tell it all, brother!"

Brother Stokes quoted Kelly Wade as having once said, "the purpose in life is to have a life." Let me say that again. The purpose in life . . . is to have a life. That was Kelly Wade.

Jerry Wilburn tells me that he visited Kelly Wade just before he died. He said that Kelly was in a lot of pain and that everyone knew his heart was about worn out. Jerry told Kelly that he loved him. True to form,

Kelly smiled and whispered, *"Everything's gonna be chicken and gravy now, baby . . . chicken and gravy."* Our communal sense of loss was deep following Kelly's death. Things weren't the same at C&P where his son Chip trudged on with the family business, or at the Pit Stop where he liked to hang out and drink coffee and watch folks pump gas, or at the high school football games where he had been a presence for nearly sixty years, hanging on the cyclone fence near the twenty yard line, urging the boys on. He was remembered everywhere. As David Cole at Itawamba Community College told me, we were all just in a big blue funk after Kelly Wade passed on. We felt somehow cheated that we would never again be dazzled by Kelly Wade's raucous ebullience. A life bottomed on love. Love for his fellow man. And I pondered for some time what meaning, if any, to apply to our lives here on earth if the final jots and smidgeons and tittles and whits of existence mean nothing more than a long final sadness. And loneliness. Like many who have lost someone close, I just couldn't shake it. Kelly Wade Prestage was simply the best homegrown personality Itawamba County could produce.

Some time after the funeral, I was driving to Court, listening to a classic oldies radio station, still brooding the loss of my friend. But a song came along, reminding me of him, and granting some peace. As these words drifted from the speakers, I thought of Kelly Wade and Linda and the joy he gave all of us:

*and if the sky . . .
we look upon . . .
should crumble and fall . . .
and the mountains . . .
should tumble . . .
to the sea . . .
no I won't be afraid . . .
no I won't be afraid . . .
just as long as you . . .
stand by me . . .*

Armis

I like good talkers. One of my favorite conversationalists was former Chief Justice of the Mississippi Supreme Court, Armis Hawkins. Armis Eugene Hawkins was born in Natchez on Armistice Day in 1920. His birth, while notable, was not the only big event of 1920. Women got the right to vote and drunks lost the right to drink. Babe Ruth hit 54 home runs that year. The first radio station in America, KDKA in Pittsburgh, Pennsylvania, went on the air. As we like to say, "A lot of water has run under the bridge since 1920."

Armis died in the Spring of 2006. A big slice of Mississippi history and a chunk of good humor passed with him. Sid Salter, the eminent editorialist for the Jackson *Clarion-Ledger,* our State's largest daily newspaper, said of Chief Justice Hawkins that he was one of those ". . . public officials who hold the public trust in their hands as if it were the most fragile piece of crystal - bright and shining and easily broken if mishandled."

Armis's father ran a store in Natchez and owned Mississippi and Louisiana plantations totaling 4500 acres. Armis' early childhood was typical for a young aristocrat. His mother saw that he had violin lessons, read great literature and listened to classical music on her wind-up Victrola. Her efforts were well-spent. Armis always enjoyed lively discussions of the works of Shakespeare, Balzac and Anatole France and relished the opera and theater. His grasp of the classics had a practical value too. He once criticized my participation in a Mississippi Supreme Court case by saying that "not since the days of Jean valJean has a man suffered such a miscarriage of justice." (I had read *Les Miserables,* thus feeling the sting.)

Standing about six feet four inches, and thin as a blade of Johnson grass, Armis Hawkins was never what we in North Mississippi call "fleshy." A boyish grin always threatened to erupt across his thin face and a shock of unruly hair fell over his forehead, hinting at nonconformism. Though he loved high-brow art and literature, Armis also appreciated the simple humor and earthy wisdom found in the life and lives of just regular common folks. He knew that simple souls sometimes state the most sublime truths. Armis gained this broad grasp of humanity from surviving the Great Depression and spending much of his life in rural North Mississippi.

The genteel life of his birth did not last for Armis. His father lost the Natchez store and all their plantations in the Great Depression. With financial loss came the loss of privilege. The Hawkins family spent the early 1930's moving from place to place . . . Kosciusko, Gibson, Belmont . . . as they sought better opportunities.

His family finally settled in Houston where Armis' mother ran a dry goods store until 1936 when she was diagnosed with tuberculosis and confined to a sanatorium. Armis now had to help support his family. He joined a Civilian Conservation Corps work camp where he was paid $30 a month for digging ditches and planting pine seedlings. Twenty-five dollars of his monthly earnings were sent home to support his family.

The young Armis Hawkins refused to surrender to the mean circumstances life had given him. He saved enough money from his meager CCC earnings to enter Wood Junior College, a small Methodist school located in Webster County.

From Wood, Armis went to Ole Miss where he studied law. His life long sensitivity to class in Mississippi is revealed by his recollections of his early days at Ole Miss. He said, "I recall the unease I felt my first night at Ole Miss hearing students roving through the Grove shouting, looking for freshmen and "bullrats," transfer students. In Memphis in 1939-40 people from Mississippi and to a lesser extent, Arkansas, had slurs made about them, although in all likelihood over half the city's population originated there. How easy it is to feel superior . . . "

Armis adjusted to college life soon enough. Returning to campus one Sunday morning, after spending a late night in Vardaman with some college friends, he learned that the Japanese had bombed Pearl Harbor. He immediately volunteered for the United States Marines.

Marine Corps training is tough, but Armis told me it was a cakewalk compared to the Civilian Conservation Corps. After a few weeks of training, Armis was sent into combat as a private in Guadalcanal, where his natural leadership abilities were soon recognized. He was transferred to Quantico where he completed Officers' Candidate School and then returned to the Pacific as a First Lieutenant where he served for the War's duration. He and his men fought all the way to Tokyo.

High-school boys across Mississippi were told during Christmas break in 1942 that if they would join the cause immediately, arrangements would be made for them to graduate when they got back from the war. One of Armis' young friends from Houston, whom I will call Johnny, joined the army during the Christmas break. Johnny fought at Iwo Jima where he was badly wounded.

Armis found Johnny in the Iwo Jima camp hospital. He took Johnny under his wing and made sure he got good medical care. Johnny's wounds were too serious to allow him to return to combat. Armis put the boy on a ship headed back to the U.S., telling Johnny to go back to high school and finish his education and that he would see him again when he too came home.

After the War, Armis returned to Mississippi and obtained his law degree in 1947. He opened a country law practice in Houston, Mississippi, determined, he told me, ". . . to rid Mississippi of Bilboism and Prohibition."

Armis often recalled a beer referendum in Houston

when the preachers and bootleggers allied to keep the small town dry.

The public schools got involved in the beer controversy and one old maid English teacher instructed her students to write an essay on "The Evils of Strong Drink." The best essay would be read aloud at one of the anti-beer rallies. Armis' friend Johnny, survivor of Iwo Jima, was in the class. A couple days later, the teacher called for the papers to be turned in. Johnny had no essay.

"Johnny," she asked, "where is your paper?"

"I didn't write it," he said.

"Why not?"

"I just cain't."

"Don't you know I will fail you in this course if you don't write that essay."

"Yes, mam."

"Well, then, are you going to turn one in tomorrow?"

"No, mam."

"And why not?"

"Lady, I done been to war. There ain't no way you nor nobody else can make me write anything I don't believe."

The English teacher failed him and Johnny never graduated from high school. No doubt the authorities acted within their rights in failing Johnny. The law was on their side. But maybe someone with a broader grasp of humanity would have seen things differently.

Armis' lifetime circle of friends went well beyond Jimbo and Johnny and me. The nationally prominent Gore family, which includes former Vice-President Al Gore, has strong roots in North Mississippi. Armis was sitting at a Gore Homecoming in a little country church in Calhoun County on a hot Saturday afternoon, listening to a preacher drone on and on, when he noticed a 'fella' seated in front of him squirming and fidgeting like a worm in hot ashes. The fellow was obviously uncomfortable. After watching the cultivated, intelligent gentleman continue to twitch and wiggle for some time, Armis leaned forward, pecked him on the shoulder and whispered, "Fella, I believe you could use a drink." The fellow, author Gore Vidal, nodded and smiled, and a long friendship between the Justice and America's most celebrated man of letters began. The two corresponded for years. Armis and his son Jim visited Vidal in Italy and Los Angeles and Vidal visited Armis in Mississippi. Armis always enjoyed recounting an anecdote about a Gore visit to the Mississippi capitol city. Liquor cannot

Armis Hawkins and Gore Vidal

be bought legally in Mississippi on Sundays. Gore was visiting Miss Eudora Welty for a very sober Sunday brunch, and after some discussion of politics and literature, Mr. Vidal said, "Miss Welty, I understand there is not a legal drink to be bought in Mississippi today. What *do* folks around here do on Sunday?"

To which the *grande dame* of Mississippi letters replied, "Why Go-ah, we go to church."

Armis served as District Attorney from 1951-1959 during a difficult time of racial unrest and Ku Klux Klan violence. His sense of fairness and dedication to the law and humanity sometimes put him in danger.

Armis drove a Chrysler New Yorker with a powerful V-8 engine in the1950's. It had no air-conditioner so Armis placed white sheets on the mohair seats to reflect the hot summer heat. He once prosecuted a suspected Klansman for a hate crime a few counties away from home. The jury finally returned a verdict late in the evening. As the involved parties were finally leaving the Courthouse, Armis noticed a couple of pickups following him. As he turned onto the highway he noticed they turned too. He sped up a bit. So did the pickups. As they came closer he noticed that the drivers of the trucks and their passengers were all dressed in white. The Klan! Shots were fired. He gunned his big Hemi engine and the Chrysler roared ahead. The pickups sped up too. They were getting closer. Suddenly they slowed, stopped and turned around. He then realized that his windows were down and his own white sheets were billowing out the windows. The Klansmen assumed he was one of their own.

Armis ran for Lieutenant Governor in 1959 as a progressive in a mean era of racial pandering. He lost the election to Paul B. Johnson, who would later "Stand Tall" against integration at Ole Miss. Following this loss, Senator Jim Eastland asked Armis to organize the slate of Mississippi electors supporting John F. Kennedy for U.S. President. Kennedy lost to the "Un-Pledged" electors by nearly 8000 votes state-wide. Following this loss Armis retired from politics for the most part and dedicated himself to his private law practice.

By 1972, Armis had fought the Japanese and the Klan, had run a state-wide campaign for public office, had dabbled in national politics, and had matched wits with some of the best trial lawyers in the South. Yet one of his most legendary battles was yet to be fought. He would be routed, like the Yankees at Brice's Cross Roads, by one Hector Brown. Armis did not accept his defeat by Hector in silence. Their skirmish is documented by the following letter from Armis to Hector.

11 August 1972

Canine Hector Brown,
c/o Honorable W. W. Brown,
Circuit Judge,
Calhoun City, Mississippi

Dear Hector:

You will perhaps recall me as the homo sapiens who was upon the Brown premises the other day. Not seeing Judge Brown's car, I intended to ring the side doorbell and deliver some papers to Mrs. Brown, but decided not to advance that far in view of your attitude. I then went around to the front of the house to press the doorbell there, but your displeasure at my being in the front yard was not perceptibly less than my entry into the back yard. Therefore, it took only the slightest cognition on my part to decide to put the papers in a gate latch — the place which presented the least apparent risk insofar as you were concerned — and make my departure as quietly yet as quickly as possible commensurate with keeping a good eye on you as I retreated. I could only hope that Judge or Mrs. Brown would notice the papers in this unusual place, which fortunately they did.

Now, Hector, I think I should take this means to speak to you quite frankly.

First, I want to commend your devotion to your Master and Mistress, domicile and territory, but especially your courage, even for a terrier. I know that if I were barehanded to be confronted at any time or under any circumstances with an animal twelve times my height and twenty times my weight, the last emotion in the world I would display would be anger. (Humans have learned a little more guile than canines, however.) It took remarkable intrepidity on your part to evidence such ferocity. You richly merit being a namesake of that noble and brave Trojan immortalized in Homer's Iliad.

It is also apparent to me that you are of some maturity, a dog who has reached the age of respectability. I can easily imagine that you are no stranger to bouts of muscle and joint aches, rheumatism, which afflict most animals of various species when they reach certain ages, but particularly dogs and humans. I could detect a certain innate irritability about you, and this comes to all of us when we have experienced enough of life's disappointments and no longer look at the world as full of wine and roses, and all that sentimental stuff. I could tell that you just do not believe in much foolishness, out of either dogs or humans.

But, Hector, I think you should thoroughly understand that I meant no harm. I did not go there to disturb your household, to wet one of your yard trees or territorial posts, or make an olfactory exam of your anus.

I went to your Master's house on legitimate business. He is a Circuit Judge, and from time to time he will have lawyers calling upon him to transact important affairs (at least to them). Haven't you noticed them already? You will find that lawyers for the most part are pretty decent folks, and mean well. After all, your Master was one once.

Now, I am going to try and get along with you, Hector. I am going to make a determined effort to remember the next time I have to go upon your premises to take you a wiener or a piece of hamburger meat. I want your friendship very much, because after all you have many admirable qualities.

This being said, however, I want to make a final observation; while I am a great admirer of your Master, and also think a lot of you, if you advance upon me again as you did the other day, and do not at the same time afford me the opportunity of retreat without loss of too much dignity, I am going to do my dead level best to part your head from your shoulders with my foot.

Yours truly,
HUMAN HAWKINS

In 1980 Armis re-entered politics and was elected to the Mississippi Supreme Court where he was soon recognized as an independent thinker. (He also continued his speeding ways. He was once stopped by a U.S. Park Ranger on the Natchez Trace who advised him that his State inspection sticker had expired. Armis told the

Chief Justice Armis Hawkins addressing Joint Assembly of Mississippi Legislature

Federal officer that, "I don't see that that is any of your business," rolled up his window and sped away. I will leave it to sharper legal minds than mine to settle the merits of that Federal-State controversy.) Armis eventually rose to Chief Justice and served until 1995 when he voluntarily retired and went back to practicing law. At the age of 75.

Armis and I became friends in the early 1980's, when I was first elected to the legislature. Houston was not out of the way from Aberdeen to Jackson, and now and again I would receive an early Monday morning call from Armis. "Fella," he would say, "you headed for Jackson this morning?"

"Yessir."

"How bout swingin' by and giving me a ride?" Since Armis was a gifted conversationalist, I was more than happy to be his chauffeur.

I drove a tiny four-speed, two-door Subaru in those days. Armis could barely get in it. Yet he never commented unfavorably on our modest wheels. He would kiss his wife Pat goodbye and we would head down the Trace. I would put on some music and we would talk our way along.

You may have surmised by now that Armis was not above recounting a good earthy tale. Some might say he had developed a bit of a taste for scatological humor. I will try to do justice to one of his favorite anecdotes. Since I first heard Armis tell this one at a rather formal dinner, I believe he and I will both survive the retelling.

Armis told a story about a little red-dirt hill county farmer and his twelve-year-old son who were plowing their spring corn with a mule back in the early 1930's. The father said, "Son, it's gettin' near dinner time. I'll go to the house and get us a bucket of biscuits and a jug of water and you hold the reins and hang on to the handles and keep plowing 'till I get back."

The day was hot and muggy and the old mule stank and attracted horseflies, and the little barefoot boy could hardly reach the plow handles but did the best he could, hanging on as the old mule lurched along between the corn rows. Now and then the mule would absent-mindedly plop a big splat of waste right in the boy's path and the child would have to jump quickly to one side to miss it. Yes, folks, this is the sort of thing that hard-working farmers had to put up with in the days before tractors.

After a couple of rows, the plow-point hit a mole tunnel. The little boy looked down, astonished at the strange little creature the plow had exposed in the hot sunlight. He whoahed the mule to a stop and picked up the mole.

The mole was fat and gray and about four inches long. The boy marveled at the creature's pink little face and blind eyes and delighted in its fat little waving hands, as though it were swimming in the air. He stood pondering the strange creature and swatting horse flies when the mule dropped a big plop right in front of the plow. The boy look at the mule's rear end and inspiration and opportunity collided. According to

Armis, only a twelve-year-old boy would have thought to do what this little boy did next. He looked at the old mule's tail lazily swishing flies, then stuck the mole up to the Mule's rear end and stood back to watch the mole's pink little hands digging away. The creature entered the mule.

The mule brayed and sat down in the corn. It then stood back up, braced its legs and jumped straight in the air. Getting no relief standing still, the mule took off across the corn patch, dragging the plow behind. Then it jumped the rail fence, hanging the plow as it headed down the sandy hollow, bucking and snorting, and dragging the fence behind.

The father returned with a molasses bucket full of biscuits and a jug of water, just in time to see his mule, plow and fence heading toward a sweetgum thicket. "My goodness! Son what's wrong with the mule?"

The little boy stood staring toward the thicket. "I don't know, Daddy. But looks like he may have a mole up his ass!"

Back during our traveling days, I listened to a good bit of old blues music. I am fascinated by the art form and its influence on today's popular music. Often as we left Houston, Armis would say, "Fella, put on some of that music," and I would slip in a tape by Elmore James or Sonny Boy Williamson or some other Mississippi artist and jabber a bit about how Delta music influenced this or that Rock-N-Roll superstar and Armis would indicate his interest. For instance, I would play *Crossroad* by Robert Johnson, which Armis said he enjoyed, and then I would pop in Eric Clapton's version and crank up the one Subaru speaker and Armis would lean his head to the dash to hear better and be greeted with a thundering DONH-DONH-DONH-DA-DONH, etc. He would listen patiently, then lean back and say "Fella, I just don't understand it," and I would turn the music down and we would move on to something else.

Armis had a favorite restaurant in Jackson, the original Monte's Seafood and Pasta, which had the best spaghetti and meatballs in the world. We enjoyed many pleasant meals there. Senator Hob Bryan sometimes joined us. On one such occasion, Armis brought a bottle of wine and we spent most of the evening discussing matters of State and other such things as you might or might not expect a Senator, a Supreme Court Justice and a lowly Representative to talk about. The conversation worked its way around to popular music and Armis said, "Senator Bryan, Representative Mills here has been trying to educate me on this modern music ... this stuff I believe you call rock and roll. Now I have been trying to understand it, but for the life of me, I can't seem to grasp its essence. I can't see what it is in the music that you young fellows seem to enjoy. Senator, maybe you can enlighten me on this new music."

Hob lay down his fork, took a sip of wine and deadpanned, "Chief, it's in the lyrics."

"The lyrics, you say?"

"Yes, the lyrics. You have to understand the lyrics if you want to appreciate Rock-N-Roll. For instance," and

Hob began flatly reciting the following words:
"I cain't git no . . .
Satisfaction."
Armis listened attentively.
"I cain't git no . . .
Satisfaction."
Armis waited expectantly for the lyrics to develop.
"I cain't git no . . .
Satisfaction!"
Armis leaned across the table, hoping for a sublime resolution to Hob's recitation of that great Rolling Stones hit. The droll Senator continued his recitation:
"Well, I've tried . . .
And I've tried . . ."
Armis knew the resolution was coming now! He leaned toward Hob and listened intently as the Senator continued:
"But I cain't git no . . .
Satisfaction!"
Armis leaned back in his chair. He had no response. I gleaned from his silence that the good man felt a bit sorry for the Senator and me. But I believe that, in the end, Armis found great satisfaction in knowing he was respected by his peers and loved by his family, neighbors and many friends.

After Armis died, one of his neighbors, Sonny Scott, wrote a letter to the *Northeast Mississippi Daily Journal* which captured the essence of one of Mississippi's great public characters. I will borrow Mr. Scott's words here:

Judge Hawkins was of another era... His was a world in which the law was codified common sense, the purpose of which was to grease the wheels of economic and social intercourse, rather than an instrument of self-enrichment for a class privileged by intelligence and training but unencumbered by morality or sense of responsibility. My mind rebels at picturing his face on a billboard asking, "Injured in an accident? Hurt on the job? Call..."

The Judge was a gentleman, but more importantly, he was a hard-working and honorable citizen. He was smarter than most of us, but he used his gifts to improve his community and state rather than preying on the productive class. He was a good old Southern Democrat, in all that was good and noble about the best of that breed...

Judge Hawkins was an imposing man in stature, and impressive in intellect, but he was humble, as befits a citizen of a republic. His home was neat and attractive, but modest. Nothing suggested that one of the State's most distinguished attorneys lived there. No scandal dogged him, professionally or personally. He was as approachable as any merchant or tradesman in town. A suitable epitaph would be, "Judge Hawkins, American."

Literacy and Hawg Hunting

I know a gaggle of governors and a handful of U.S. Senators; a bunch of judges and a fair number of legislators, mayors and county officials, among others; and Sut-N-Goober.

I like to run with folks who have a lot of spunk, some devilment and a bit of curiosity about life. Folks who aren't afraid to ponder the big questions. Who am I? Where am I going? And when does duck season begin? These are some of the important questions I discuss with my special friends, the boys in the Tombigbee River bottom. These cheerful stoics take no prisoners in our round-the-campfire discussions of life. A quick wit and thick skin are as essential to survival on the banks of the old Tombigbee River as Carhardt breeches and Mossy Oak sweaters. We leave dogma and ideology and such to folks who don't laugh a lot. Stiff-lipped characters who have all the answers may get their feelings hurt in our crowd.

But I am not just a river bottom guy. I can hang with the reading and writing crowd too. Writing seems to be second nature to many of my contemporaries. My law school classmate, John Grisham, is one of the most widely read authors in history. He is not my only former classmate to be a successful writer. Judge Jim Fraiser, now of Tupelo, turns out a book about every three weeks. My dear friend, Jim McCafferty has published several short stories and children's books. Circuit Judge Bobby DeLaughter has written a moving account of his prosecution of DeLa Beckwith, the murderer of Medgar Evers. Another Ole Miss buddy, Martin Hegwood, writes a novel about every six months. I envy their energy. Good writing is hard work.

I will accept about any excuse to get good people together. Books often give me that opportunity. I began a practice when I was in the legislature and on the Supreme Court in Jackson, of hosting little "readings" of my friends' recently published works. I would cook up some beanie weenies and slice some cheese and put out the crackers and get some napkins and invite friends over to hear my friends read from their works. (I still owe Grisham a reading. His buddies in the legislature bought most of the first edition copies of his first book, *A Time to Kill*, when he was selling them out of his trunk. It never occurred to us at the time to have a reading. We were just trying to help John out.) Of course, invitees to the readings had to buy a book, and the authors graciously agreed to autograph their published materials for my guests. As time went on, these meetings began to occur quite frequently, due in large measure to Fraiser's profligate writing habits. And the crowds grew as word traveled. These get-togethers were never a nuisance. I will always treasure the good friends made and the wonderful conversations heard at our readings.

Back in the late 1970's, I moved and restored an old log cabin in the Peaceful Valley community in Itawamba County. Over the years, this cabin became a gathering place of sorts for my band of free-spirited friends. A few years ago, I bought another little shirt-tail piece of property adjacent to my cabin and lying along the old Tombigbee River. The land wasn't worth much. Its primary value to me lay in giving my sons, Chip and Penn, a place to hunt. At the time of purchase, I was unaware that two characters named Sut and Goober came with the property.

Folks in Itawamba County know Sut Sheffield (we pronounce it Shurfield) and Goober Dozier as two of the best hawg hunters to ever tromp around the Tombigbee River bottoms. I first met them one cold December afternoon when they came stumbling out of my woods dragging an eight-point deer and a young hog between them. Goober is tall and wiry with a long white beard and hunts in tan cover-alls. Sut is shorter and stouter and has hunted in the same torn camouflage since I first met him.

Sut-N-Goober reminded me of the Biblical Moses paired with a South American freedom fighter creeping, well-armed, out of the approaching darkness. Not to be intimidated by these trespassers, I introduced myself as the new owner of the property. They accepted this news kindly enough and patiently explained to me that they had hunted this land all their lives and knew that I would be just delighted for them to continue to help me keep varmints off my place. Being politic by nature, I assured them that I was more than happy to have their assistance. Thus, I got into the business of hawg hunting.

The Tombigbee River bottoms are full of wild hawgs. They are not only numerous, but damaging to the ecology. A rooting, snuffling drift of hawgs can obliterate, in minutes, the small wheat and clover food plots we tend year round for deer. I've seen food plots that look dynamited after a single hawg attack. Now when I say hawg, I'm not talking about cute little Porky Pigs. Our critters are low-butted, big shouldered razorbacks. Their thick chest hair is matted into a briar-proof and bullet-resistant shield. Some have sharp tusks over eight inches long. Wild hawgs are smarter and tougher than any other woodlands creature and can outrun a deer. And some of them are mean. They will eat anything, dead or alive. When I learned they were destroying my young wild turkey population, I began to insist on the regular presence of Sut and Goober on my small bottomland property.

Sut-N-Goober are superb woodsmen. They both have public jobs to be endured, but their true joy is found roaming in the thickets and "scopes" and hollers of the Tombigbee River bottoms. A walk through the woods with Sut-N-Goober is like reading a good novel. I don't talk much when I follow them for two reasons. One, I am trying to learn. As we pass through a grassy embankment on the river, Goober might say, "Look where that doe slept last night." I will look and see nothing. Sut will then add, "Yeah, and her baby slept over there." I will look and again see nothing. As we plunder on, Goober will say, "Look where that 'coon dug up a yeller jacket's nest layst yeer." I will look and see nothing but a faint indentation in the leaves. As we crowd through a cane break, Sut may remark, "Well, it looks like a hawg came through here two weeks ago. I would say he was about knee high." To which Goober may respond, "Yeah, and he had another one with him. A little spotted shoat." I will look and see nothing but chewed weed stems and scratched cane and the faintest of trails. They read the woods. The second reason

Goober Dozier, Sut Sheffield and wild hawg

Literacy and Hawg Hunting 195

I don't say much around Sut-N-Goober is because I recognize my own limits in the presence of greatness.

Let me digress from hawgs and speak a minute on the subject of hawg hounds. Goober favors the big shouldered yellow hounds known as black mouth curs. These dogs are loyal, intelligent and courageous. Anyone who has watched the movie *Old Yeller* will be familiar with black mouth curs. Sut prefers a shorter, stouter hound that resembles a bulldog. He dresses his hounds for success. His dogs are quite cute laced in the little orange Kevlar vests to protect them from hawg attacks. Our gang makes a bizarre sight stumbling through the bottoms on a frosty December morning, some of the dogs in bullet-proof vests and most wearing collared radio transmitters beeping signals to the tall mantis-like aluminum antenna waved by Goober as he dodges through the woods.

Hawgs can get in the darndest places. I've seen Goober crawl thirty yards through brambles and briars and six-inch thorns that a rabbit couldn't enter and drag a squealing ninety-pound shoat out by its hind legs. Goober prefers to save shotgun shells and usually cuts a big hawg's throat with a butcher knife. The younger ones he will castrate on the spot and turn loose for fattening.

Well, a couple of years ago, when word got out of my impending appointment to the Federal court, some of my Itawamba friends suggested a "cooking" at the cabin. This crowd included the usual Itawamba wits, Brad Chatham and Jeff Reeder; my cousin Honest Don

Dulaney; and others of lesser note. Goober came to the occasion even though he was on crutches because a really big boar hawg had recently gored his knee. Nevertheless, he honored us with his presence and sat quietly in a chair, listening to the give and take of country repartee.

My friend Brad Chatham is a carpenter by avocation and also has a degree from Daytona Speedway in small engine repair. He analyzes human nature as well as Mark Twain or Will Rogers. Reeder is a certified mechanic and world class tinker. Both are gifted story tellers. Honest Don mostly cooks and cleans up.

Some say clothes make the man. I am not sure if they make the hunter. Our circle enjoys a wide range of sartorial splendor. Jeff Reeder is fetching with his hunter-tan Australian bush hat and color-coordinated boots. His pressed Mossy Oak shirts and breeches always match. Brad usually wears a faded green Notre Dame football sweater covered with dry wall dust. My hunting outfit consists of a camouflaged Wal-Mart T-shirt someone gave me and ragged blue jeans. Honest Don doesn't even pretend to hunt and dresses accordingly.

Well, as events would have it, Jim Fraiser had written a flattering article about my permanent departure from Jackson soon after news of my pending appointment to the federal court became public. Jim's article was published in that big town paper, the *Tupelo Daily Journal,* and the boys from Itawamba County, or at least some of them, had read the article in which Jim had somewhat exaggerated my contributions to the artistic community of Jackson. He was kind enough to bemoan my leaving but wished me well in Oxford. His comments about my "readings" let the cat out of the bag as far as the boys from the bottom were concerned.

After we had eaten and shared some tales around the fireplace, Brad, innately aware of where to stick a needle, brought up the matter of my "friends in Jackson" and wanted to know why I had never brought any of them to the cabin, implying, of course, that I did not want to mix my "uppity" bookish buddies with my hawg hunting friends. Reeder and Honest Don alleged that they too had read the article and also questioned why I was reluctant to bring my Jackson city friends to the bottom. Goober offered no comment either way but sat silent and sage in the rocker. Little did they know that I had been waiting for an opening to discuss some things that had been on my mind. Brad's inquiry gave me the opportunity I had been seeking.

I shushed them all, including two aspiring musicians who were hanging around. B.J. Canup and John McLeod, unrequested, were entertaining us with their vocal and guitar tributes to the *Oh Brother, Where Art Thou* soundtrack.

I stepped to the center of the hearth and sized up my audience. Virgin territory. I responded to their digs by saying that I had given a great deal of thought to the fact that my two circles of friends had remained so distant and, now that it appeared that I would be in north Mississippi full time, I was going to have to change some of the rules regarding attendance at the cabin. Since it was unlikely that my Jackson friends could come up to north Mississippi very often, I was handing down a new edict that each hawg hunter must read a book and give a report on same at each of our future meetings. (I thought, if nothing else, this would certainly clean up the attendance.) Sensitive to the fact that perhaps Goober might not be as familiar with reading literature as others in the group, I stated a corollary to my edict that Goober would be exempt from this rule. I nodded toward Goober, seeking his approval, but he sat passively, offering no thanks. Undeterred, I turned to the other members of the audience and said, "Now that we know the rules, let me give you a short lesson in literature."

I began my narrative. Unaware of the seriousness of my presentation, Reeder stepped up beside me on the hearth and, holding his hands behind his back to warm them before the fire, began jabbering about that "big basket-racked, blue-bottomed buck" he had missed for the third time in two years. He had seen it again that afternoon in the bottom and stated that it was "coming at me so fast I felt the wind blowing as it knocked down sweet gum saplings in its path. I thought a storm had hit." I interrupted him, and somewhat irritated said, "Jeff, this is exactly why we don't have book reviews at the cabin. Your attention span is about as long as a rooster's pecker. Now, if you don't mind keeping your anecdotal bull to yourself a few minutes, I would like to have a rudimentary discussion of literature."

He fussed a bit but backed away from the hearth and let me continue. Canup chose this moment to tune his guitar. "And that goes for you too, B. J. I am determined that you folks are gonna think about literature just this once. Now put that guitar down!" He did.

I looked back at my audience who now sat quietly, eyes cast downwards as though intently studying cracks in the floor. I repeated that, in the future, I would assign, prior to each Saturday night cookout, a book for each hunter to read. I again nodded toward Goober and winked fraternally and stated that "real hawg hunters" wouldn't be expected to read anything. "The rest of you boys, though," I said as I shifted my gaze from face to face, "will be required to do your assigned reading and must be prepared to intelligently discuss what you have read." As an afterthought, I added, "You will also be expected to help Goober and me actually hunt some hawgs, as will also be required of any of our friends from Jackson who might in the future visit us here." Having established these ground rules, I proceeded to discuss my opinion of literature. I noticed Reeder now had the bottom of his boot twisted across his lap toward the ceiling. He was studying it intently.

I told the boys that I had recently had a conversation with Jim Fraiser in Jackson. We were discussing literature and I stated that I hadn't read a lot of Shakespeare but had read an awful lot of William Faulkner, and was of the opinion that Shakespeare and Faulkner were dipping from the same well. Fraiser caught my drift and replied that he suspected they may have been the same person. I said that after my discussion with Jim, I had read an essay by a fellow named Richard Bloom who posited the notion that Shakespeare created modern man. Not in the sense that he formed us out of dust, but in the sense that in his numerous plays and sonnets, he was the first writer to capture individual human intellect and emotion. I blessed my listeners with Bloom's theory, and feeling like I was on a roll, stated that of all the writers I had read, I thought there were only four really great ones. Shakespeare, of course, and then Herman Melville, who wrote *Moby Dick,* one of the grandest books I have ever tried to read. "After you read it," I said, "I believe you will agree with E.M. Forster that *Moby Dick* is much more than just a great fishing story."

"Is E.M. any kin to the Forsters over in Tilden?" Honest Don asked.

"No. E.M. Forster wrote *A Passage to India.* Another book we might read. And besides, you are referring to the 'Fosters' in Tilden. Not the 'Forsters.'" I sighed to myself, "Ah, humanity!"

I returned to my audience, again nodding toward Goober, and stated that I did not expect all of them to read Melville. However, I said that I thought some of them could read Melville, and if so, they would discover a strong similarity between Shakespeare, Melville, and our own William Faulkner. I then said that for many years I thought the line of genius had ended with Faulkner but, lo and behold, I had recently begun reading books by one Cormac McCarthy, who is still alive, and, like Faulkner, is a southern writer. I told the boys that I had determined that the flame of genius glowed yet again. I wound up my narrative by stating authoritatively that next week I expected each of them to be prepared to present a short discussion on one work by any of these four authors: Shakespeare, Melville, Faulkner or McCarthy. I assured them that I was looking forward to the discussion. Not wanting to make him feel uncomfortable, however, I turned to Goober and said, "Goober, since you provide the dogs and most of the meat, I will again exempt you from having to read any of these authors."

Feeling rather pleased with myself, I nodded toward the group for their response. No one replied. They just kept staring at the floor. I could feel a bit of embarrassed tension developing. Finally, Goober looked up from his chair, and fixing me with a certain cold indifference usually reserved for a bayed shoat, responded to my condescending lecture by stating in his flat, honest, country dialect, "Well, I'll admit that I might of done a lot better in high school if English hadn't a been so tough. But if that feller you're talkin' about had wrote a book about a *Great White Hawg*, I might of read it."

They looked at me grinning, awaiting my response. Of course there was none. I had been ill-prepared for this unexpected but very public denouement. I stepped down from the hearth, thereby relinquishing the floor, and muttered to myself, "Well, call me Ishmael!"

Nine-One-One

I had been re-elected to my fourth term in the Mississippi Legislature in November of 1995 when Governor Kirk Fordice appointed me to a position of Justice on the Mississippi Supreme Court. I replaced my friend, retiring Chief Justice Armis Hawkins. I was at my post on the Supreme Court in the Summer of 2000 when I received a telephone call from Mississippi's senior United States Senator, Thad Cochran.

A little more about Mississippi politics and politicians. We all know each other, usually on a first name basis. Thus, our beloved Senator Thad Cochran is simply " Thad" to most Mississippians. Likewise, Senator Lott is known as "Trent." I will remain true to this practice in my narrative. Thad told me that he and Trent had received a letter from District Court Judge Neal Biggers alerting them that he would be taking senior status. Senior status is a fancy term that means semi-retired in the federal judiciary. By taking senior status, Judge Biggers was making it possible for the Northern District of Mississippi to get an additional judge.

Thad said that he and Trent had discussed the appointment between themselves and that they had checked with our mutual friend Jerry Wilburn, and wondered if I would be interested in this position. Would I? The job meant not only that I would receive a substantial pay raise. I would also be able to re-enter the courtroom. As a trial judge, rather than an appellate judge, I would be interacting on a daily basis with lawyers and jurors and real people, rather than trying to find five votes to get out an appellate opinion. The job had other attractions. As a federal judge, I would be located in Oxford, Mississippi . . . The Modern Athens . . . The Little Easy . . . Intellectual Hub of the South. . . . I told Thad that I thought I would be very happy with such an appointment. He said, "Well, if you are interested, I will submit your name to the President."

I wasn't sure what he meant by "submit." "Do you mean you will submit my name, along with others, to the President?" I asked.

"I mean," he said, "that we will submit *your* name to the President. But don't give up your day job yet. We have an election to go through and we won't know until November who the President will be."

In fact, we did not know in November who the next President would be. It was nearly Christmas before we learned that the next president would be one George W. Bush.

Between the Fall of 2000 and the Spring of 2001, the newspapers were filled with rumors and conjecture as to who would be appointed to the Northern District

Judgeship. Many fine names were mentioned. Mine wasn't. I knew that several powerful lawyers and businessmen in North Mississippi were sponsoring various other folks for the position. While I would have enjoyed having my name on the speculative list, I didn't give this oversight much thought. I knew Thad and Trent operated on their word.

Sometime in January 2001, I received a call from the Oval Office in the White House. I was told that our Senators had in fact submitted my name to President Bush and that the President's Chief Counsel, Alberto Gonzalez, would like to meet with me at the White House.

One might infer from later national press accounts that I was selected because I was a wild-eyed saboteur of the Constitution. In truth I was never asked one question by Mr. Gonzalez or anyone else on the President's staff that could be construed as ideologically biased. Mr. Gonzalez's main inquiries concerned how I would relate to lawyers in the courtroom.

Alberto Gonzalez, who is now U.S. Attorney General, showed me around the Presidential offices and kindly took my picture in the Rose Garden. I also visited Senator Cochran's office and met a delightful Washington journalist, Barbara Olson, who told me of a new book she had coming out.

While I was at the White House, I was asked to provide all of my telephone numbers, home, work and cell phone, because, I was told, the President liked to talk to his nominees personally before formally nominating them to the Senate.

Following my meeting in the White House, I underwent intensive F.B.I., Secret Service and I.R.S. background investigations and passed a required physical. (I didn't know I had poor vision, a kidney stone and partial loss of hearing in one ear until the Federal government had me checked out). Other than passing these medical tests and background checks, I wasn't very concerned about my nomination process since Trent was President of the Senate and his friend, Republican Senator Oren Hatch, chaired the Senate Judiciary Committee. In southern vernacular, we had the big dogs on our side. We anticipated an early Spring confirmation hearing before the Senate Judiciary Committee. No one could have foreseen that Republican Senator Jim Jeffords of Vermont would declare himself an independent, thereby ending the Republican majority in the Senate and throwing the Senate leadership into disarray. His action caused all of the Bush judicial nominees to be put on hold as the Senate was forced to reorganize under new leadership.

Mona and I and the kids were attending the Mississippi Bar Convention in Destin, Florida, in July of 2001 when I noticed on my cell phone that I had missed a call. I didn't recognize the odd number and therefore didn't immediately return the call. Later that day, when I had nothing else to do, I rang the missed-call number, primarily out of curiosity. To my surprise, the President's Oval Office secretary answered and told me that President Bush had attempted to call me earlier. She said she was sure he wanted to talk to me, that he was in an important meeting at the time, and could he call me later at the same number? *WHAT you say, scannel-bugger!* Of course he could call me back at the same number!

I assured the President's secretary that I would stay near that number for the rest of the day. I then noticed that my cell phone reception was less than two bars in the condo. Good reception on the Coast at the time could only be had at the water's edge. It is hot and sunny at the water's edge. But there I stood for the next two and one-half hours, holding my phone heavenward, waiting for one of the most important calls of my life.

I was cooked a fairly pink, medium, well done by about 4:30 in the afternoon, when my cell phone buzzed. I nervously answered. It was the President's secretary.

"Would you like to hold for the President?"

"Certainly." *(Does a hawg like mud?)*

President Bush introduced himself over the phone and told me he was happy to nominate me for the United States District Court for the Northern District of Mississippi. He seemed genuinely pleased, thereby making me feel very special. I suspect that the President thought I was much older than him, due to the fact that he referred to me as "Sir" a few times in our conversation. Or, perhaps he is that kind of fellow. I have no idea what I said to the President, but I can tell you that President George W. Bush's enthusiasm is contagious and I was deeply flattered to be his nominee.

We were soon notified that my hearing before the Senate Judiciary Committee would be on September 13th, 2001. Mona and I were to fly to Washington on the afternoon of September the 11th. My meeting with the Department of Justice to prepare for my hearing was to be held on the 12th. Things didn't go according to plan.

I awoke in Fulton, Mississippi, on September 11th, 2001, fixed a pot of coffee, as was my habit, and turned on CNN. I was shocked by what I saw. The newscasters were showing film of a big passenger airliner hitting one of the World Trade Center Towers. It appeared to have been a horrible accident. Like millions of Americans, I watched in horror as men and women jumped from the towers to escape the flames bursting from the windows. Incredibly, the scene got worse.

Most of America watched as another plane crashed into the second tower. We then heard that a third airplane had hit the Pentagon and that yet another had gone down somewhere in Pennsylvania. The events were too co-ordinated to be accidental. We soon heard the name "bin Laden." The shock of learning that a human agency was behind the carnage filled me with an intense sense of loss and anger at such an audacious exhibition of pure evil. My feelings were echoed by New York City Mayor Richard Giuliani who said, the loss was "more than we can bear."

One of our founding fathers, Alexander Hamilton, is

buried in Old Trinity Church cemetery in New York at the intersection of Broadway and Wall Street. I had visited his grave earlier in the Summer. It is fitting that the remains of our first U.S. Secretary of the Treasury should be buried at the end of Wall Street. Among our founding fathers, Alexander Hamilton was most responsible for our capitalist economy and dedication to free markets. Our personal, religious and economic freedoms were targeted on September 11th.

I watched as the towers finally collapsed, killing thousands and saw thousands more innocent people stumbling in the streets, numb with shock. They were soon overtaken by a huge hot gray cloud rumbling down Wall Street, coating all in its path with poisonous dirt and destruction. At that moment, these words came to mind:

nine-one-one
i saw ashes fall . . .
like dirt gray snow,
on Hamilton's grave,
at Old Trinity . . .
i choked . . .
and tasted tears
of innocents
blown dry
on grayed
canyon walls . . .
as hot angry
winds

*proclaimed
our Nation's
rebirth . . .
and loss of
innocence.*

Within the hour, we learned that no air travel would be allowed in the United States for an indefinite period of time. I was unable to contact Senator Cochran's office and heard nothing from the Department of Justice. My affairs seemed rather petty, considering the emergency facing our nation. Mona and I did what millions of other Americans did on that day. We called Alysson at Ole Miss to check on her and gathered the other children, Penn, Chip and Rebekah, around our dining room table and did something we had not done in a long, long time. We prayed.

The Dow-Jones stock exchange was closed, not to be re-opened for several days. All commercial and private air flights were cancelled and grounded. Schools across the nation were closed. America was stunned. Somehow, we had to go on. Later that afternoon, I joined my junior high spelling coach, Miss Eupal Thornberry and her 'Young at Heart Club' for a special service at the East Fulton Missionary Baptist Church. Going to Washington now was the farthest thing from my mind.

On the morning of September 12th, Brad Prewitt, chief legal counsel for Senator Cochran, called and told me, "If you can make it to Washington by tomorrow, we would like to hold the hearing." I was surprised to hear this but told him I would be on my way. At midday on September 12th Mona and I left for Washington, D.C., not knowing if our country would be attacked again. The world had changed. There was little traffic on the roads. There were no airplanes in the sky, except U.S. Air Force jets on patrol. All radio stations were giving complete coverage to the disaster. No music was to be heard on the air. It was a time of sorrow. We were encouraged by stories of heroism and courage as accounts of individual bravery were reported on the air and touched by accounts of survivors being found in the rubble. I was saddened to learn of the death, in one of the airplanes, of Barbara Olson, whom I had met earlier in the year.

Mona and I saw the American spirit being reborn as we traveled from Fulton to Huntsville to Chattanooga to Knoxville to Virginia and through the Shenandoah Valley into Washington D.C. Tiny American flags began sprouting in yards and on bridge sidings; in front of churches and above businesses; and sometimes just along the road. It was as though we were following a modern Johnny Appleseed, leading us to Washington by planting red white and blue symbols of freedom. The little flags were the voice of a proud people waking from a national nightmare. We were coming together again.

We drove 16 hours straight, facing black smoke rising from the Pentagon as we rolled into Washington.

I napped in Brad Prewitt's apartment and then headed to the Capitol where Thad and Trent introduced me to the Judiciary Committee. The meeting was chaired by Senator Patrick Leahy, the senior Senator from Vermont and co-chaired by Senator Mitch McConnell from Kentucky. Senator Joe Lieberman and Senator Orrin Hatch were there along with others. Four judicial hearings had been set for that day but only Judge Barrington Parker from Connecticut and I were able to make it in time for our hearings.

In all fairness to the Senators and others involved, I don't believe anyone's heart was really in the hearing. The Senators were courteous and their questions were meaningful. However, I had the sense that I was simply a very small part of an effort being made by millions

Glenn Davidson administering oath to Judge Mills as Mona looks on

across the country to just put one foot in front of the other and somehow keep going and show the world that we would not back down. We were doing our jobs despite the atrocities suffered on the 11th of September.

After my hearing, Senator Leahy said he would like to speak with me privately. We chatted a few minutes and he said that he suspected my nomination would easily go through the Senate due to the respect that he and others had for our Mississippi Senators. He paused a moment and then asked how Southerners were reacting to the national tragedy.

I told Senator Leahy that I thought the people of the South would respond more patriotically than any other part of the country. I predicted our people would go to New York by the thousands to help recover bodies; deliver supplies; provide medical services; and begin the rebuilding effort. I told him of the little flags I had seen sprouting along the way.

I continued:

> *I think these events, as painful as they may be, will heal our nation of much regional strife. For too long we have been divided between North and South, East and West. We will come together. For we in the South see that New York is our city, too. It doesn't belong only to New York. Or to the North. It is an American city. And the Pentagon is our Pentagon too.*
>
> *It occurs to me, Senator that this is the first time a Northern city has been attacked by for-*

eign forces. We Southerners understand your sense of loss and we share the nation's sense of loss because in Mississippi our Capitol was burned to the ground in the Civil War. It became known as Chimneyville. We lost Atlanta. We lost Richmond. We lost . . . so much. This sense of loss is part of our heritage. We grow up knowing it. We share it with you today. An attack on New York is an attack on us. Today we are all Americans. And we are enraged.

A Few Final Words

Some chapters in life, like stories in a book, are more climactic than others. Some years stand out in memory. Such times are the markers and milestones by which we measure our lives. The year and its dates recall the excitements, griefs or joys of a brief moment or a series of events. In retrospect, we see that changes that seemed so undesirable, obstacles that appeared so insurmountable, at the time, were, in fact, a necessary process of renewal. Hindsight sometimes reveals purpose in life's patterns.

In August of 2005 Mississippi watched helplessly as Hurricane Katrina reduced her coastal communities to rubble. In the early hours of August 28, from the safety of our homes in north Mississippi, we watched the storm seemingly inhale and exhale, expand and shrink, and finally devour grand casinos and little bungalows alike. We sensed the devastation although we had not yet witnessed it.

A couple days after the winds retreated, I spoke with my old legislative buddy, Representative Warner McBride of Batesville, who lost his father-in-law in the storm. Warner, his wife Phyllis, and their three sons had gone to the coast with a bulldozer and supplies to help in rescue and care efforts. I wanted to help too. Our court family in Oxford quickly assembled a trailer load of bottled water, bleach, canned goods and other necessities. Many of my friends, whom you know from these stories, gave money and supplies, including Jerry Wilburn who donated several hundred gallons of diesel fuel. U.S. Marshals Kelly York and Jeff Davis volunteered to escort me to the Coast.

We hauled our load along the Natchez Trace to Jackson and then along such roads as were available. Flat tires were a problem from Jackson south since the winds had blown roof shingles and nails across the landscape. The National Guard had cleared trees from the main roads but downed power lines laying across the roads were common. Occasionally a store would be open, lighted by a single bulb running off a gasoline generator. Inside the stores one smelled the stench of rotting food from the defrosted frozen goods.

We found Warner and Phyllis at the home of Billy and Lorraine Cuevas, just north of where the little community of DeLisle used to be. A number of storm refugees and volunteers were camping in and around the Cuevas home. Lorraine, Phyllis and Polly Cuevas and other women worked wonders cooking rice and red beans on a single butane burner, feeding their two dozen or so guests. It would be two more weeks before they could hold a funeral for Phyllis' father, Mr. Horace Necaise, Jr., who had died while placing other family members in a live oak tree where they survived the hurricane. Warner later described the funeral service as "forlorn." Mr. Necaise was buried among toppled tombstones and debris, which included a barge and a Volvo, in the battered cemetery.

The Mississippi Gulf Coast is about 90 miles long. For nearly the entire length of the Coast, and for three or four miles deep, we found absolute devastation. It looked like an angry giant had stomped the coast. Barges, boats and casinos rested on the highways and railroads. Towns and villages had disappeared. Garbage and junk of every description hung in the trees and covered the ground. Automobiles were wrapped front bumper to rear bumper around some of the old live oak trees which, up and down the coast, had survived Katrina's fury. The old trees were leafless and haggard but still standing. By contrast nearly everything man-made was gone.

I spent much of my free time during the next twelve months delivering trailer loads of food stuffs, electric heaters and building materials to the coast. Some who rode with me on various trips include Judge Susan DelPesco from Delaware and Parker Howard and John Daniels of Greenville. Others who accompanied me were Don Kilgore and Bill Burnett of Batesville, Becky Moreton and Corbin Cox of Oxford, Baker Martin and "Big Show" Johnson of Aberdeen, and my sons, Penn and Chip. Brad Chatham led a team of Itawamba County folks, including his son, Colin, and his construction foreman, JoJo Johnson and my long-time friend,

Bill "Tutti" Love. The Chatham Gang tore out and replaced damaged sheet-rock for the uninsured poor and elderly. Mona's mother, Betty Jean Robinson, and her aunt, Tootsie Wardlaw, worked in temporary kitchens.

The year 2005 marked, in my mind, an important milestone in my life. That year I turned 49 and lost both my father and my father-in-law.

I have lived most of my life handling things myself. Early success at anything, like winning a spelling bee, breeds more success. Continued success often leads to independence. Independence sometimes causes us to give ourselves a bit too much credit for what we may have been given in life. Outer trappings of success, such as nice cars, big houses and official titles, may overshadow the importance of cultivating a strong inner life. Times of stress expose our faults as surely as storms test standing timber.

After my father died in April, I felt an awkward emptiness. I wondered why I was unable to mourn, and I prayed for relief from what I can only describe as tired numbness. I received no answer to my prayer. I finally looked to the heavens and said, "I give up." I thought no more about it.

A day or two later, between lying down to sleep, and just before my head hit the pillow, I felt a real, palpable touch from an unseen hand, as though something beyond being had brushed softly against me, faster than a twinkle, waking me to an awareness that all creation is surrounded by an ocean of love. I knew at once who had touched me. For at that instant I remembered a little boy with a flat-top haircut standing in a graveled parking lot, looking heavenward in fear and wonder, more than forty years ago.

Three months later Mona lost her father, whom we affectionately called PeeWee. He closed his eyes on July 4 and died holding the hands of his wife and children. Before he died, PeeWee loved to watch the weather, as all old men do. Maybe he was attuned to its effect on his joints and his emphysema. But I choose to believe his fascination with the forces of nature had something to do with his reverence for the Almighty. I wonder if, had he lived only a couple of months longer, he would have watched Katrina's wrath with the same admiration he gave a rainstorm.

After Hurricane Katrina, coast residents reported spring-time blossoming in October and November. Azalea bushes and lemon trees eerily bloomed at Christmas. The old live oaks, which have stood against so many storms, put out new leaves. Nature zealously responds to disaster. The disorienting spring blooms are necessary for the plant kingdom's survival. We are no different.

When blessed with time to reflect, it sometimes happens that, almost involuntarily, our mind sorts through the debris and clutter of our lives and we stumble upon some meaning. Accounts of such profound moments are as old as time. The young man, Elihu, told Job that God might speak once, maybe twice, to a person and that we may fail to recognize him. I like to think that

God spoke to me and anyone else who was listening in 2005. For 2005 brought belief in the midst of disaster . . . belief in heaven awaiting those who passed on . . . and belief in the hearts of those who remain to finish the work we have begun.